# SYNCOPATED GRACE

# SYNCOPATED GRACE

## TIMES AND SEASONS WITH GOD

LINDA J. VOGEL
DWIGHT W. VOGEL

UPPER ROOM BOOKS®
NASHVILLE

Cover and Interior Design: Thelma Whitworth
Cover Photo: © Kevin Schafer/CORBIS
First Printing: 2002

#### Library of Congress Cataloging-in-Publication Data
Vogel, Linda Jane.
Syncopated grace: times and seasons with God / Linda J. Vogel and Dwight W. Vogel.
    p. cm.
Includes bibliographical references.
ISBN 0-8358-0978-1
1. Christian life—Methodist authors. I. Vogel, Dwight. II. Title.
    BV4501.3 .V64 2002
    248.4—dc21                                                    2002002107

Printed in the United States of America

*To*

*Taylor and June McConnell,*

*wise mentors, valued colleagues,*

*precious friends*

*who embody the rich treasures*

*of God's amazing syncopated grace*

*and*

*in memory of our*

*beloved grandson,*

*Caleb Jeremiah Pulver*

*(February 22, 1976–February 25, 2002)*

# Contents

# Introduction

We were sitting around the table after sharing a delicious meal with good friends. They knew we were going to take a sabbatical from our teaching responsibilities at Garrett-Evangelical Theological Seminary and would be writing another book together. "What's the new book about?" they asked.

We told them that the book would answer this question: How can we learn to recognize the presence of God as God breaks into our lives in both expected and unexpected times and seasons? We stated our belief that life is composed of intersecting rhythms, some predictable and others surprising. By looking at these rhythms through the lens of the sacramental, we hope to help readers become aware of them as grace-filled encounters with God.

Jim Purdy remarked, "That sounds like syncopation to me." The two of us looked at each other, grabbed a paper napkin, and wrote down *syncopation* as we responded with excitement, "That's our title: *Syncopated Grace!*" Thanks to Jim, we've let that title guide us in our writing.

While both of us have done a good deal of writing for publication, we hadn't written a book together until

*Sacramental Living: Falling Stars and Coloring Outside the Lines,* published by Upper Room Books in 1999. The process we discovered in writing that book worked again for us in writing this one. One of us would begin a chapter and write as long as thoughts kept coming. Sometimes we wrote notes to each other: "Story needed here" or "This needs rewording." Then whoever had started passed the computer disk to the other person, who proceeded to revise, edit, add, and subtract. We handed the disk back and forth, then read aloud to each other. Only when we deleted a whole paragraph did we keep it in a backup file for future reference (and we ended up never going back to that file anyway!). As in our last book, the final text is "ours," not a gluing together of "Dwight's" and "Linda's."

We continue to be convinced that Taylor McConnell is right in teaching us that stories are not merely illustrations, but the foundation from which propositional truth comes. Again we have heeded Tex Sample's advice to us years ago: "Mine your own experience." One of the highest commendations of our last book came from readers who told us, "Reading your book was like having a conversation with you in person." We hope this will be true again.

Many of the stories in this book come from our own family experiences. We were blessed to have extended conversations with many colleagues and friends while writing this book: Taylor and June McConnell, Jack Seymour and Margaret Ann Crain, Jim and Mary Purdy, and Paul and Carol Clark. Their insights extend far beyond the specific citations included here.

Again we are grateful to the community of learning at Garrett-Evangelical Theological Seminary for providing the sabbatical time for writing this book. Our students and faculty peers continue to teach us much. To all who support theological education there, we say a heartfelt "thank you."

Finally, we give thanks to God, who continues to gift us with syncopated grace over and over through family and friends and acquaintances, through the community of saints known and unknown, and through the church and the world. To God be all the glory!

# Persistent Patterns

*Moments of grace, epiphanies, and great insights are lost to us
because we are in too much of a hurry to notice them.*
—Frederic and Mary Ann Brussat
*Spiritual Literacy*

A clock ticks. Day breaks and evening falls. Thursday
and Friday are followed by Saturday and Sunday. Spring
gives way to summer; autumn heralds the approach of winter. February ends and March begins. Between the last day
of December and the first day of January, we turn a page of
the calendar and discover ourselves in a new year. Academic
terms come and go; graduating classes move on. In the life
of the church, Easter follows Good Friday. All these are persistent patterns with a steady and expected rhythm. They do
not surprise us but provide a basic beat by which we can
measure the passing of time, milestones to mark our journey.

In this relentless and reliable rhythm, we experience
times and seasons that do not follow the expected patterns.
They have their own dynamic, syncopated rhythms, unlike
the steady beat behind them. In music, syncopation is the
temporary shifting of the musical accent from the usual
pulse (beat) to a place that surprises the ears. Both the
steady, underlying pulse and the unexpected, offbeat
accents are part of syncopation. Likewise, God's grace

comes to us through both the persistent patterns that form the pulse of life and through experiences that break into that pattern.

Sometimes the syncopated rhythms hold so much significance for us that the underlying, persistent patterns become barely discernible. When lovers look into each other's eyes, they forget the ticking of the clock. During the first days of loss and grief, the hours hardly seem to move. Yet time does move on; we are aware of both the power of immediate experiences and the persistent patterns behind and around them.

Life is composed of intersecting rhythms, some predictable, others surprising. Some are so life-changing that they disrupt any sense of order or natural movement of life. How can we learn to recognize God's presence in both expected and unexpected times?

## Rhythms That Make Life Human

As we began writing this book, spring was trying to nudge winter out of the way, and winter was resisting with all her waning might. Yet we know that one season follows another. Spring will come, even though we may have to endure one more snowstorm before her blossoming glory finally arrives. Still, spring does come; day is born from night; and as daylight dies away, night returns.

So days and seasons come and go; years pass; and we are surprised to discover that retirement will soon be upon us. We were gifted with three children; now our granddaughters have children, and we are great-grandparents!

Patterns mark our lives. Our infant children become adolescents and, before we know it, our young adult children are middle-aged. Abraham and Sarah begat Isaac, and from before that time until today, generation follows generation. Some of the sustaining rhythms of life mark the linking of generations—our legacy from those who have gone before and our connection with those who are yet to come.

As a pueblo dancer observes: "When you are dancing, all the sound vibrates within you. Your body becomes one instrument among others, a part of the whole. Through this we become joined to creation, to those who have gone before and to those who are yet to be."[1]

Driving down a lane past a deserted barnyard off a country road in Wisconsin, our daughter and her husband found a private family cemetery. They located the graves of Dwight's great-great-grandparents, the Erffmeyers, there and were excited to share their discovery with us.

Dwight's great-grandfather, the son of those great-great-grandparents, went to Kansas as a circuit-riding missionary. His eldest son had a daughter who married a preacher. They had Dwight, who was ordained in Kansas before moving to Iowa and then Illinois to continue spreading the good news of Jesus Christ. Family patterns, often part of the undergirding rhythm of life, help us know who and Whose we are.

Times and seasons come in many forms. Some are based on the earth's cycle of seedtime and harvest, summer and winter. Others are based on the activities of adults and children—the school year, summer vacation, baseball season, tax season. We call some retired persons from the north "snowbirds" because they go south for winter. One season marks their leaving; another marks their return.

Individuals may mark life patterns on their birthdays or by their membership in the class of 2002 (or whatever year). Sometimes we mark our life patterns by achieving a position at work, committing to a life partner, having children, ending a committed relationship, finding ourselves with an empty nest when the last child leaves home, becoming an orphan with the death of our parents, or embarking on a new chapter of life with retirement.

People of faith experience rhythmic patterns as they remember the key events in their particular faith stories. Christians experience seasons of the church year, from Advent and Christmas to Lent, Easter, and Pentecost.

All these patterns can slip into the background of daily life, and we may not pay much attention to them. Then a surprise in the pattern jars us into consciousness. A thirtieth, fiftieth, or seventieth birthday may unsettle us so much that we become depressed by the passing of this milestone. But we may also joyfully celebrate these marker events in the patterning of our lives.

Our heartbeat sustains us from its first beat after our conception until our final breath. When that life-giving rhythm fails, we experience arrhythmia, and drastic action is required to sustain life.

Life for individuals and communities also has its persistent patterns. Our friend Mary Purdy calls these rhythms "the cadence of life"—the drumbeat marking the passing of times and seasons. No matter how much attention we do or do not pay to the patterns forming our lives, these rhythms move under us and around us to provide the structure out of and into which we live.

A Santa Clara Pueblo woman, Tessie Naranjo, finds patterns in nature to which all humans are connected. She says, "Movement is life. Without movement, change, and transformation, there would be no life or death. Movement is seen everywhere. The clouds rise out of the mountains and move across the sky, forming, shifting, and disappearing. The clouds become the model for the way people need to move through life."[2]

## Rhythms That Make Life Sacramental

Times and seasons can also come to have deeper meaning for us. To understand the depth dynamic at work in that process, imagine three circles:

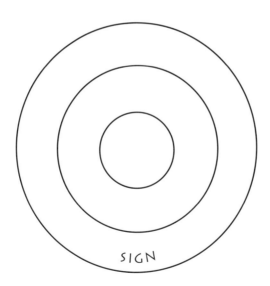

*Signs* point to something. In June 2001, we traveled to St. Joseph, Missouri, to celebrate the one hundredth birthday of Dwight's Aunt Esther. A birthday points to the day of a person's birth, which for Aunt Esther was June 5, 1901. The date reminds us of her family of origin and their life on a farm in northwest Missouri a century ago.

Christmas is also a sign. Our celebration every December 25th points to the birth of Jesus in Bethlehem more than two thousand years ago. It reminds us that the inn was already full and that Jesus had to be born in a stable. Even people with the most secular celebrations of Christmas know that the holiday points to something religious.

"Pointing to" is all that some signs do. But some signs do more than point. They also enable us to participate in the event toward which they point, thus becoming *symbols*.

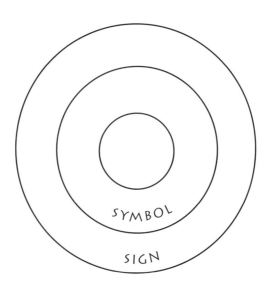

Aunt Esther's one hundredth birthday did not merely point to her birth on June 5, 1901. In celebrating her birthday, we also celebrated her life. We entered into the deep love she has given her family. Through our celebration, we participated in the depth dynamic that caught us up in seeing the ways we have become who we are because of who she is.

Shortly after Dwight's birth, Aunt Esther took the train to Ponca City, Oklahoma, and cared for him day and night for six weeks. She has always been present with her care and her prayers for him, then for us, and finally for our children and their children. She can no longer read or do handwork, has no interest in television, and is bedfast in a nursing home. While she longs to go home to God, she spends time every day remembering and praying for all of us. Our lives are powerfully entwined with hers. She shows us how to trust in Jesus no matter what life brings.

Christmas does more than just point to the birth of a baby in Bethlehem many years ago. Because it invites us to participate in giving to others, Christmas becomes a symbol. Since the baby Jesus was born in poverty, we are called to reach out especially to the needy. In Dickens's story *A Christmas Carol*, Scrooge's nephew affirms that Christmas is "a good time: a kind, forgiving, charitable, pleasant time: the only time I know of, in the long calendar of the year, when men and women seem by one consent to open their shut-up hearts freely, and to think of people below them as if they really were fellow-passengers to the grave, and not another race of creatures bound on other journeys."[3]

Signs do not automatically become symbols. Christmas

may remain an event that does not involve us in its deeper realities. Even worse, Christmas can be perverted so that it becomes a symbol of the opposite of its inner meaning. Christmas can invite us to become concerned primarily with receiving rather than giving, with lavish consumption rather than concern for the poor, with harboring resentment rather than fostering forgiveness. And all too often, it does that. We may recognize that we are not really "keeping Christmas" but abusing the event toward which it points. When Christmas loses contact with the birth of Jesus and the self-giving love his life embodied, it cannot adequately symbolize the meaning of the event. Then it is not sacramental.

Sometimes signs become symbols by encouraging us to participate in the event toward which they point. Some symbols become *sacramental*.

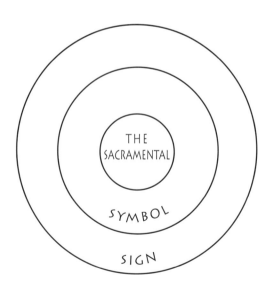

What do we mean by *sacramental*? How does the sacramental help us understand our lives? How can we learn to see the spiritual depth dynamic we experience when God breaks into our ordinary ways of thinking and doing? What makes both persistent patterns and times of "syncopated grace" sacramental for us?

Most Christians encounter the word *sacrament* in reference to baptism and the Lord's Supper. Roman Catholics also see confirmation, ordination, marriage, reconciliation, and anointing as sacraments. Beyond these ritual experiences of the church that we know as the sacraments, however, we find a broader meaning.

When we say times and seasons can be sacramental, we mean they can become *unusually translucent experiences that open us to experiencing God.* That is, they not only point to something (the quality of signs), but they enable us to participate in a deeper reality (the quality of symbols). Thus we get in touch with what lies beyond, beneath, behind, or within the times and seasons we experience. Occasionally we see through these experiences to God, who is behind and in them. When this depth dynamic includes *recognition of the sacred, an awareness of the presence of God,* we speak of it as sacramental.[4]

Paradoxes characterize the sacramental. If we have eyes to see and ears to hear, we can find the sacred in the ordinary as well as in the extraordinary. William Carlos Williams, a poet and a physician, is said to have carried a small notepad with him every day. Written at the top were these words: "Things I noticed today that I've missed until today."[5] Approaching each day expectantly—both the overly familiar and the new—opens us to receiving God's steadfast, surprising grace.

The sacramental is both *hidden* and *revealed*. One can look at Christmas and describe it superficially without referring to its symbolic nature; thus its sacramental nature is hidden. Certainly, Scrooge's attitude toward Christmas was superficial before he encountered the spirits of Christmas—past, present, and yet to come!

But to "those who have eyes to see and ears to hear" what lies beneath outward observances, the witness of the biblical narrative and the tradition of the church year testify that Jesus' birth reveals the coming of Emmanuel—God with us. Christians find in Christmas the seed that blossoms into the church at Pentecost. Christmas can be sacramental.

The sacramental is thus both *perceived* and *received*. We must learn how to look beyond the obvious and see what is really there. When we see, our response becomes, "What can I give?" We discover that God has been at work all along, inviting us to recognize the sacramental as both gift and response.

Further, "the sacramental is embodied and present in the world we experience—it is *immanent*. At the same time, the sacramental opens for us the mystery of God, who is beyond all our experience—it is *transcendent*" (emphasis ours).[6]

Times and seasons can be *sacramental* when they involve a recognition of the sacred, an awareness of the presence of God, which is

- both *hidden* and *revealed*,
- both *perceived* and *received*,

- both *gift* and *response*, and
- both *transcendent* and *immanent*.[7]

When we look at Christmas through the lens of the sacramental, it is more than a holiday; it becomes a holy day when we are aware of God's presence and action in the world. Hidden behind Christmas trees and stockings and jingle bells is the revelation that "to you is born this day in the city of David a Savior, who is the Messiah, the Lord" (Luke 2:11).

We come to perceive that we have received a great gift, and we celebrate as part of our response to that gift. Even as we participate in festivities, we celebrate the awareness that God is present to us here and now (thus, *immanent*). So we sing "O come to us, abide with us, our Lord Emmanuel!"[8] At the same time, we believe that this God who is with us is also the God above and beyond us (thus, *transcendent*): "Christ, by highest heaven adored; Christ, the everlasting Lord. . . . Veiled in flesh the Godhead see."[9]

We know that Christmas can be sacramental for us— when we really keep Christmas. We experienced a sacramental Christmas this year as we helped serve a hot meal on a bitterly cold night to the men who spent that night at our church's homeless shelter. After they ate, we visited with them and gave each one wrapped gifts—gloves, socks, scarves, and hats. In their words and smiles, we experienced a sacramental Christmas. We remembered a baby in the manger of a stable and pondered how often there is no room in our inn. We also experienced God's sacramental gift as we celebrated Christmas morning with two of our three children and their families in our Chicago home.

A less obvious fact is that celebrations of other times and seasons, such as birthdays and anniversaries, can also be sacramental. Standing around Aunt Esther's bed in her nursing home room to celebrate her one hundredth birthday, we could not (nor would we want to) ignore the way God-consciousness has consistently characterized her life. From her earliest memories, she has looked to Jesus as Lord and Savior as her firm foundation. Those aware of that dynamic cannot celebrate her birthday without recognizing the sacred, God's presence, both in her life and in our celebration of it.

Many would say she had a hard life. Her father, a German patriarch, believed that as the only daughter it was her responsibility to stay home and help care for her parents. He discouraged any suitors who came along, and she was an obedient daughter. Grandpa was killed in a haying accident. After Grandma and Aunt Esther gave up the farm and moved to town, Grandma was frail and then bedfast for seventeen years. Aunt Esther washed and ironed clothes for other people so that she could stay home to care for her mother. Her patient, tender care of Grandma was an amazing gift. Then not too many years after Grandma died, Aunt Esther's knees gave out, and her brothers moved her into a private home where she could be cared for. Her caretaker became ill, so Aunt Esther had to move into a nursing home. After several falls, she is totally bedfast. Her mind is good and her spirit is strong, but her siblings and peers are gone, and she has little reason to keep on living. As her birthday drew closer, she continued to say, "I may be here, or I may be gone. Either way is fine with me."

The sacramental nature of her birthday celebration is both *hidden* and *revealed*. Some who sent cards and came to visit only marvelled that they knew someone who was one hundred years old. The sacramental aspect of Aunt Esther's birthday was hidden from those who were aware only of external realities. But to those who could see beneath the surface to the faith that permeates Aunt Esther's life, God's abiding presence was revealed. What we saw was a gift, for her life and her witness embody faith.

When all of her siblings and most of her friends have "gone on to glory," Aunt Esther wonders aloud why she is still here in her bedfast state with knees that only cause her pain. But then she quickly says, "The good Lord must not be ready for me yet. But one of these days I'll go home to glory, and then things will be different!" Even as we celebrate her life, we continue to honor her by praying that God will soon take her home, for this is her deepest wish. And when that day comes, we will join with our children and Dwight's cousins and celebrate her coronation.

The gift of Aunt Esther's life and faith called for a response from our family, a response to the God present both in her life and in our celebration. It also called us to examine how we go about living our lives—in thanksgiving for the love she has so unselfishly given to us. Her life is "hidden with Christ in God" (Col. 3:3). To celebrate her birthday at its depth was sacramental because it invited us into God's presence and transformed our ways of seeing— our perspective.

The sacramental nature of special times like Aunt Esther's one hundredth birthday can also be true for

- the mundane meanderings of life,
- the disruptive discords that come our way,
- the revealing resurrection moments that break in upon us,
- the resonating rhythms that keep those moments of mystery alive,
- the times of sabbath rest and renewal, and
- our experiences of Pentecost power.

In the chapters that follow we want to bear witness to how certain times and seasons have been sacramental for us and how we believe they can be sacramental for you. But first we need to explore one more crucial characteristic of the sacramental.

## Harmonies of Grace

We describe an athlete or a dancer as graceful. When someone deals with a difficult situation with sensitivity and compassion, we often say "she (or he) handled that with grace." What do we mean?

Grace is a quality that we may recognize when we experience it; yet it is difficult to define. It goes beyond the expected. Grace is a special kind of gift that blesses us with presence, beauty, compassion, or care. Sometimes grace gifts us with the courage to face challenge and to risk. Sometimes it gifts us with the ability to say no or yes to a task that seems beyond our capacity.

Grace cannot be calculated; when we seek it, it eludes us; we can receive it but not store it. It is superabundant and cannot be earned or merited.

We sometimes assume that grace is a gift—"a free gift with no strings attached."[10] "Barrington Bunny," a short story that speaks to children of all ages, helps us imagine how wonderful grace is. However, it emphasizes the "free gift with no strings attached" so much that one might miss the other side of the paradox—even though it is present in the story.

Barrington bemoans that he is a lonely bunny; as far as he knows, he is the only bunny in the forest. He whines that he can't go to the squirrels' Christmas Eve party because he can't climb trees, and he can't go to the beavers' Christmas party because he can't swim. When Barrington tries to ask the forest mice if he can come to their party, they are making so much merriment that they don't even hear him. Poor Barrington is as sad as sad can be.

Then a large gray wolf comes and stands nearby. The wolf asks Barrington why he is sitting in the snow, and Barrington pours out his heart, saying, "Because it's Christmas Eve, . . . and I don't have any family, and bunnies aren't any good to anyone."[11] The wolf assures Barrington that being a bunny "is very good indeed . . . because it is a gift that bunnies are given, a free gift with no strings attached. And *every gift that is given to anyone is given for a reason*. Someday," the wolf says, "you will see why it is good to hop and to be warm and furry" (emphasis ours).[12] Thus, the story illustrates that grace is both free and binding.

All gifts call for response, and the gift is offered, even if we do not choose to receive it. But when we choose to reach out and take a freely offered gift, we are responding. The idea that grace is freely given with no strings attached has caused a good deal of mischief among Christians because we have failed to affirm at the same time that grace is "given for a purpose" and that it calls forth a response from any who choose to receive it.

Every gift obligates. One cannot receive a gift without incurring the obligation of some return gift as a sign of gratitude, even if it is only a "thank you," the bowing of one's head, or a firm handshake. Such return gifts, however, must be a free response or they don't count.[13] Ungratefulness reveals a lack of grace in one's life. Recognition of the presence of the sacramental entails accepting its claim upon our lives and responding with faith and hope through transformed living.

Our recognition of the sacramental in times and seasons transforms how we live and how we sculpt God-filled meaning to sustain us. When we accept God's grace, we are called to present our bodies (and our lives) as "a living sacrifice, holy and acceptable to God" (Rom. 12:1). We are not to "be conformed to this world, but [to] be transformed by the renewing of [our] minds, so that [we] may discern what is the will of God—what is good and acceptable and perfect" (Rom. 12:2).

Let's turn our attention to our everyday meanderings and discover how these might be syncopated with grace. How can sacramental living open us in both expected and unexpected ways as we listen to the rhythms that undergird our human experience and call us toward grace-filled encounters with God?

# Notes

1. We found these words, by Tony Chavarria of the Santa Clara Pueblo in New Mexico, inscribed on a wall at the Museum of Indian Arts and Culture in Santa Fe (April 2001). They are also found in Joan K. O'Donnell, ed. *Here, Now and Always: Voices of the First Peoples of the Southwest* (Santa Fe, N.M.: Museum of New Mexico Press, 2001), 40. Reprinted by permission of the Museum of Indian Arts and Culture and the Museum of New Mexico Press.

2. Inscribed on a wall at The Museum of Indian Arts and Culture in Santa Fe, New Mexico. Also included in *Here, Now and Always,* 30. Reprinted by permission of the Museum of Indian Arts and Culture and the Museum of New Mexico Press.

3. Charles Dickens, *A Christmas Carol* (Cleveland, Ohio: World Publishing Company, n.d.), 13.

4. See Dwight W. Vogel, *Food for Pilgrims: A Journey with Saint Luke* (Akron, Ohio: Order of St. Luke Publications, 1996), 6.

5. Quoted in Frederic and Mary Ann Brussat, *Spiritual Literacy: Reading the Sacred in Everyday Life* (New York: Scribner, 1996), 53.

6. Dwight W. Vogel and Linda J. Vogel, *Sacramental Living: Falling Stars and Coloring Outside the Lines* (Nashville, Tenn.: Upper Room Books, 1999), 24.

7. Ibid., 20–25.

8. The last line of the last stanza of "O Little Town of Bethlehem," written by Phillips Brooks in 1868.

9. From "Hark! The Herald Angels Sing," written by Charles Wesley in 1734 and altered by George Whitefield in 1753.

10. Martin Bell, *The Way of the Wolf: The Gospel in New Images* (New York: Ballantine Books, 1968), 6. The complete text of Bell's short story, "Barrington Bunny," was downloaded from http://pubweb.acns.nwu.edu/~dba330/barrington.html.

11. Ibid., 5–6.

12. Ibid., 6.

13. See Louis-Marie Chauvet, *Symbol and Sacrament: A Sacramental Reinterpretation of Christian Existence,* trans. Patrick Madigan and Madeleine Beaumont (Collegeville, Minn.: The Liturgical Press, 1995), 99–109.

# Mundane Meanderings

*The ordinary is precisely God's way of working miracles.*
*What we call ordinary is as miraculous as the extraordinary,*
*though we do not see it thus because we are used to it.*
—Ernesto Cardenal
*Abide in Love*

Let's begin with the everyday ordinary, where we spend most of our lives. Ordinary time may seem quite uneventful; routine is the name of the game. It is a time for doing what needs doing, for keeping on with the pattern of keeping on. Day follows day, week follows week. On the surface everything seems the same. Sometimes these everyday, ordinary times are comfortable, and sometimes we may feel like we are on a treadmill—going nowhere.

Boredom and great weariness may characterize our treadmill times. The repetitiousness of life may weigh us down. We feel as if there is nothing new under the sun, and our joy has been replaced by a feeling of emptiness. Somehow our lives seem to lose any sense of direction or purpose.

Not only is this true for individuals, but it also marks some seasons in the life of faith communities. A congregation may feel stuck in a rut, engaged in repetition of routine that has become empty, its life no longer *sign*-ificant. The routine seems to point to nothing at all beyond itself.

One congregation had reached this point with its huge annual rummage and craft sale. When the time came to plan the sale, church members' lives already were filled to the brim and spilling over. Someone had a grace-full inspiration. He gathered a small group who approached members one by one, asking, "What would it be worth to you *not* to chair the rummage sale next year?" they asked. "What would it be worth to you *not* to have to chair the food table next year?" "What would it be worth to you *not* to have to make ten birdhouses for our craft sale next year?" Before they knew it, they had received pledges matching last year's total income from the annual event.

On the other hand, the ordinary everyday may not be insignificant. Great comfort can be found in the familiar. Knowing the routine, the usual order of things, frees us to attend to other things. Because we can count on our daily routine, we may have energy for creative endeavors.

Frequent travelers, who from the outside appear quite free of the requirements of routine, often have patterns of behavior on which they ground their lives. They need an underlying sameness in their lives even if they sleep in many different cities and hotels. They may religiously follow the same routine as they get up or go to bed, pack their luggage, attend to personal hygiene, call home at a certain time, or have their morning coffee or their afternoon tea. Chances are that somewhere in their otherwise tumultuous days a pattern provides stability.

Identifying those patterns that keep us going enables us to attend to them consciously so that we can be sure they continue to provide us with life-giving support. We can appreciate these patterns by recognizing how they make us feel at home when we are away from home and how they undergird our well-being when we are at home.

Patterns are also important in communities of faith. At the church Dwight served in Martelle, Iowa, you could count on the church's having a Christmas Eve service and an annual men's pancake supper. One event is on the traditional liturgical calendar, and the other one isn't. But both events are part of the normal rhythm for that congregation and for the surrounding community.

St. Luke's United Methodist Church in Dubuque developed a tradition of celebrating Mardi Gras during worship on the Sunday before Ash Wednesday; they followed the worship service with a Cajun meal. In the life of that congregation, this celebration ranks close to Christmas Eve and Easter Sunday. It is a time for jazz, praise, and dancing in the aisles. But the celebration also reminds everyone that Lent begins on Wednesday. Ashes and introspection will replace the dancing.

Worship that leaves us always wondering what to do and when to do it may result in our being more interested in the superficial externals than the events to which they point. Even congregations that do not use bulletins or follow a particular order in their worship services tend to do things a certain way. People do not function well over time if they don't know what is happening or what they are expected to do next.

Brain research reveals that we are "hardwired" to respond to ritual. In other words, part of what makes us human is the capacity to develop patterns of behavior as the foundations for our lives. The basic pattern of worship enables us to attend to the ways God addresses us. Patterns themselves are not bad or good; what we do with those patterns renders them meaningful or meaningless.

The unchanging parts of a worship service are called "the ordinary"; they are what we ordinarily do. If we pray the Lord's Prayer every Sunday or sing "Praise God, from Whom All Blessings Flow," those are parts of the ordinary for us. If the service always (or almost always) begins with an organ prelude or with singing praise choruses, gospel songs, or favorite hymns together, that will be part of the expected pattern we rely on. If the order changes, someone needs to tell us, or we find ourselves embarrassed to be standing when we should be sitting. Change can frustrate us. Frustration doesn't mean that we are just old "sticks-in-the-mud" who want our way. Rather, it indicates our recognition that the patterns on which we rely provide a *sign*-ificant context for religious experience.

Praying the Lord's Prayer, whether individually or corporately, is a good example. The words are almost too familiar. When someone invites us to "say" the Lord's Prayer, that's exactly what we do—we start the tape and let it run from memorized preconditioning out of our mouths, giving little thought to what we say. But if we do not know the Lord's Prayer by heart, if we have not prayed it so often that it is second nature, those words will not be available when we really need them—when our capacity to find words of our own is reeling from crisis or fear. In fact, Gabe Huck says that it is what we can "do by heart" (not only from memory but with our inner being) that makes worship significant.[1]

One of the powerful ways our seminary community experiences the Lord's Prayer is by praying it aloud, using the "language closest to our heart." Because our community includes people of many different cultures and languages, each of us attends to our own words. Praying in our various languages reminds us that the church of Jesus Christ indeed transcends culture and language, and yet we are one.

Occasionally while we "say" the Lord's Prayer, one or more of its petitions comes alive in our consciousness. It becomes a cry from our deepest being, and we pray rather than say the words. The words we pray and sing week in and week out need not be vain repetition. But given the nature of human habit patterns, we will have times when the words are merely mundane meanderings for us. Sometimes when we feel like our prayers are bouncing off the ceiling, praying the Lord's Prayer in community is all that holds us together.

We highly underrate the extraordinary nature of the ordinary. Just as breathing and heartbeats provide the basic rhythm for our bodies, so the basic patterns of our living can be channels of God's grace to us. Monastic communities treat the rituals of rising in the morning and retiring at night as calls to prayer. To awaken to another day is gift; to commend ourselves to God each night places us within the basic pattern of life, of all that is begun, continued, and ended in God. We too can be sustained by prayer when we awaken, at mealtimes, and before we go to sleep.

Sometimes just putting one foot in front of the other is itself a victory. When life seems chaotic, we fall back on those basic patterns, and often only then do we recognize the grace they carry. When we see someone who no longer knows what to do next or how to do it, we long for them to recover the gift of ordinary routine. At times of deep loss and grief, our underlying patterns of being and doing carry us through when we don't feel like we can go on.

Sitting in the sunroom of an Alzheimer's wing of a nursing home with a group of eight Roman Catholic women, Linda saw them pray the rosary together—moving their beads and their lips. Although the women could not do anything else in community, this lifelong routine seemed to bind them together and affirm that, even in this diminished state, they were valued children of God. This was a sacramental moment for Linda. We believe it was sacramental for these women of faith as well—though we cannot know for certain.

At times we become acutely aware that God is in the ordinary, though often unrecognized, unheralded, unappreciated. Sometimes the veil lifts, and we awaken to the sacramental potential of the mundane: sharing a cup of tea with someone, sunlight on the wall in the morning, water to drink, food to eat, seeing the first robin after a long winter, going to worship on Sunday morning as our custom is. The season of the everyday ordinary can be sacramental indeed if we pay heed. It is good that this potential exists, for most of us spend a great deal of our lives in the mundane meanderings of life.

One danger of meandering in the mundane is that we may *see only what we know*, which blocks us from *knowing what we see*. Jesus demonstrated that he recognized this danger when he asked his disciples: "Do you have eyes, and fail to see? Do you have ears, and fail to hear? And do you not remember?" (Mark 8:18).

Another danger of mundane meandering is becoming blinded by unexamined assumptions. Life becomes a self-fulfilling prophecy. We "see" what we expect based on how we have experienced situations in the past. We need to discover with Ernesto Cardenal that "all things are very mysterious and strange . . ., and we overlook their strangeness and their mystery only because we are so used to them."[2] Learning to know what we see is an important step toward experiencing God in our mundane meanderings.

In her book *Everyday Sacred,* Sue Bender describes the journey she took because she "felt a hunger inside" that she "didn't understand and couldn't satisfy."[3] She admits hoping for a "big miracle," but in the end she realized that the answer she sought was to be found in her discovery that "small miracles are all around us. We can find them everywhere—in our homes, in our daily activities, and, hardest to see, in ourselves."[4]

We must not discount our mundane meanderings. They challenge us to look for God in the most unexpected places—to recognize God's presence with us as we hug a child, as we make cookies for a church bake sale, or as we rush to get dinner on the table because of family members' various commitments that evening. God is with us even when we feel unappreciated at work and when the laundry doesn't get done.

All of us who use computers have experienced times when we were ready to heave them into the bottom of the sea! Computers are unforgiving, and they don't have an ounce of common sense. After a most frustrating encounter with her computer, Sue Bender finally concluded, "Nothing is wasted time. If I can learn from a mistake, then it is not wasted time. The only mistake is to not learn from a mistake."[5] Even when we find ourselves sinking fast into the mundane, in our most frustrated states, we can learn lessons and claim insights.

When we keep our eyes and ears open as we meander in the mundane, we can stop and look again so that we get beyond our assumptions. Beyond what we expected to see, we may find "God-incidences"[6] that bless us every day.

## Wandering in the Desert

Sometimes those meanderings take place in the desert. In these seasons of wilderness wandering we seem to have lost our way. We may not know where we are headed, or at least, we don't know how in the world to get there. We are no longer on the direct route, the fast track. Maybe our initial goal no longer seems desirable. Or perhaps we still value it, but it no longer looks attainable. Whatever the reason, we find ourselves in directionless territory with no map or compass. Or maybe our map is so outdated that it seems useless, or our compass clearly is malfunctioning.

A key biblical image of wandering is found in the story of what happened to the Israelites after the Exodus. They set out for the Promised Land. Life did not turn out the way they planned; they ended up wandering in the wilderness for forty years. They must have wondered if there was life beyond wilderness wandering; for a whole generation of Israelites, there wasn't.

This story contains important keys for survival in the desert. One key is to realize that water and food are available, if you know where to look. When you find them and recognize them as God's gifts—as water from the rock and manna from heaven—desert wandering can become a sacramental season.

Reflecting on the Israelites' exodus wanderings makes us think of the Burren, a strange and wondrous area on the west coast of Ireland. Approaching this coast, a visitor sees what appear to be great barren limestone hills—dark, forbidding, inhospitable. The Irish tell a story about General Ludlow, who served with Oliver Cromwell in the seventeenth century. Ludlow said of the Burren: It had "not enough wood to hang a man, not enough water to drown a man, nor enough clay to bury a man, clay is so scarce they fight over it, yet their cattle are fat."[7]

This last observation—"their cattle are fat"—provides a clue that the Burren contains more than one sees at first. Even though the land looks barren from a distance, the limestone rock is covered with crevices containing a large variety of little plants. These crevices retain water for a long time, and the rock absorbs enough heat from the sun so that the unique Burren vegetation persists throughout the winter. While soil in the lowlands is often cut up by cattle hooves, the rock of the Burren resists trampling and protects its fragile plants. Hence, in spite of all evidence to the contrary, "their cattle are fat."

Learning to trust is another key for survival in the deserts and wilderness areas where we find ourselves. Dwight sings a folk song about a desert wanderer who is

parched with thirst and comes upon an old rusty pump. The
thirsty traveler finds a note in a baking powder can attached
to the pump; it directs him to a jar of water hidden under a
nearby rock. But the note warns its finder not to drink the
water. Instead, it says to use the water to prime the pump,
promising that the well contains plenty of good, cold water.

What should the wanderer do? Drink the warm water
from the can because "a bird in the hand is worth two in
the bush," or trust the unknown person who left the water
and the note that the traveler's thirst will be more than sat-
isfied? The wanderer decides to trust and pours the water
into the pump. And as the people of Israel did when Moses
followed God's instruction to strike the rock with his staff,
he enjoys an abundance of good, refreshing water.

The early monastic movement recognized that the
desert contained refreshment for parched souls. Individuals
went to the desert to pray and meditate, and there they
found spiritual clarity. When Dwight served as pastor of St.
Luke's United Methodist Church in Dubuque, Iowa, he followed the advice of his bishop, Rueben Job, and took one
day a month as a "desert day"—a day of silence and meditation away from the busyness of life. Oh yes, the desert
contains food—food you cannot find anywhere else.

The story of Israel's wilderness wanderings contains
another truth: Sometimes we discover God's gifts in the
wilderness. At Mount Sinai the descendants of Abraham
and Sarah received what became for them the most precious of all of God's gifts—the Law, summarized in the Ten
Commandments. Thus, the wilderness became the site of
the greatest mountaintop experience recorded in Hebrew

scripture. Holy times may have their context in seasons of wilderness wandering.

Sometimes in our wandering we find that "the journey is our home."[8] When Moses led the Hebrews out of slavery in Egypt, he certainly could not have imagined that they would wander in the wilderness for forty years and that Joshua, not he, would lead the people into the Promised Land. Moses' entire life consisted of wilderness experiences—as a baby born to slaves in Egypt, as a child raised in an alien culture as an adopted son of a princess, as a fugitive with murder charges hanging over his head in Egypt, and as an outsider in Midian where he married and tried to settle down.

But God had other plans, and Moses returned to confront the Pharaoh and demand, "Let my people go." Then for forty years Moses led those murmuring, backsliding ex-slaves in their wilderness wanderings. How amazing it was that God chose murmuring, backsliding ex-slaves to bless and call as a light to the nations.

The other great wilderness story of scripture takes place just after Jesus' baptism. Mark 1:12 tells us: "And the Spirit immediately drove him out into the wilderness." Luke 4:1 puts it more gently: "Jesus, full of the Holy Spirit, returned from the Jordan and was led by the Spirit in the wilderness." Either way, wilderness wandering clearly is not a God-forsaken season. God's Spirit—whether demonstrated as a pillar of fire or felt as a presence—indeed goes with us into the deserts and wildernesses of our lives.

Jesus' experience in the wilderness reminds us that the wilderness offers plenty of temptations that try to divert us from a path of faith and hope. We are tempted to trust only in ourselves, to put our trust in the untrustworthy, and to claim more for ourselves than is ours to claim. Fear, anger, despair, and blame seem to surface when we find ourselves in the desert places of life. Taking matters into our own hands, as Aaron did when he made the golden calf, is another temptation to avoid.

The Holy Spirit may lead us into the wilderness, sustain us with food we do not know is present, and perhaps (although not inevitably, as we learn from Moses' experience) lead us out again. When we dare to trust the Spirit to lead and guide us, we will find blessings even in the hard places of life. And even when the experience has an ending we could never have envisioned or wanted, we may, like Moses, have another mountaintop experience and see the Promised Land.

Spending time in the wilderness teaches us that we cannot rely only on ourselves. It requires us to recognize our inability to be self-sufficient. When we find ourselves away from the busyness of life and from our preoccupations and diversions, we are more likely to come face-to-face with who and Whose we are. Desert times almost always call us to reexamine our perspectives and priorities.

Congregations also face times of wilderness wandering. Occasionally they set seemingly impossible goals. For example, a congregation builds a multipurpose room as the first stage of a larger building, but the membership does not increase. So the single room must function as fellowship hall, classroom space, and worship center, and it doesn't adequately address any of these needs. The congregation seems to be caught "wandering in the wilderness" with the Promised Land not even on a distant horizon.

Consider the story of Epworth United Methodist Church in Chicago, our home congregation. Once an affluent church with many well-to-do members, Epworth had a large sanctuary with a three-manual organ and beautiful stained-glass windows, a fellowship hall with a fireplace, a gymnasium/auditorium, and a lovely chapel. But eventually the neighborhood changed: parishioners died or moved away, and a small group of people found themselves worshiping in the chapel. In the sanctuary, plaster was falling and broken windows had to be boarded up. The cost of upkeep had become prohibitive; and the church plant, formerly the congregation's pride and joy, had become an albatross to the remaining members. The church's original goals and mission were no longer relevant. Survival became the primary concern, for the death of the congregation seemed just around the corner.

A former student of ours pastors a church with an aging congregation that doesn't want to reexamine its mission to the neighboring community. She says, "I feel like what they want is a chaplain in a hospice unit, someone to help them die." And sometimes dying is the only option. Is God present in the midst of desert times and places like these?

The testimony of scripture and the story of many congregations would answer this question with yes. Just as our personal experiences contain more than meets the eye, so it is in congregations: Coming to recognize God's presence in the desert can enable us to survive. Our desert times may prepare us for the idea that someone else may reach the Promised Land for which we yearn. Our task may not be to get there but to keep the vision alive.

Wilderness wanderings can be sacramental seasons when we become aware that God will not forsake us, that God will provide a way where there seems to be no way, and that even if we die in the wilderness, God is with us. If we trust in God, our desert times can richly bless us.

However, we cannot ignore the difficulties of the desert times of life. We may feel abandoned and lost. In the midst of it all, water may come from the rock, streams may flow in the desert, manna may come from heaven, and God may be made known on the mountain. Somehow we survive and so we sing:

> "Fear not, I am with thee, O be not dismayed,
> for I am thy God and will still give thee aid;
> I'll strengthen and help thee, and cause thee to stand
> upheld by my righteous, omnipotent hand.
>
> "When through the deep waters I call thee to go,
> the rivers of woe shall not thee overflow;
> for I will be with thee, thy troubles to bless,
> and sanctify to thee thy deepest distress."[9]

## Seasons of Searching

Along with the everyday ordinary and wilderness wanderings, mundane meandering may manifest itself in at least one other way: as a sacramental season. Times of searching may become sacramental.

Our meandering ceases to satisfy. We yearn to find our way. We search relentlessly. The problem is that sometimes we don't know what we are looking for.

Life has times when spiritual amnesia sets in. We know there must be something more to life than we have found, but we don't seem to have a clue as to what it is. Even when we succeed in our occupation, live in a nice home, and have a number of acquaintances, still we lack fulfillment. Much of the current interest in spirituality results from this kind of searching. We feel the need for something more than the material world can offer, a spiritual "something."

We may be tempted to try one spiritual fad after another in an effort to find that "something." Not knowing what we are looking for, however, makes it difficult to know it when we find it! Nonetheless, we think, *I don't know what I'm looking for, but I'll know it when I see it.* And despite the problems of such a search, that position holds some truth. We may have heard someone speak of the "God-shaped hole" in our soul that nothing else can satisfy. When God seems unreal to us and we don't know who God is, we can't know much about that God-shaped hole, let alone what might fill it.

Perhaps we search for something we cannot achieve by human effort. Maybe we do know what we seek: the experience of God's presence, a grace-filled life "hidden with Christ in God," or peace that the world cannot give. We know what we want, but we don't know where or how to find it.

Sometimes we look so hard for answers that we cannot recognize clues along the way. During our search we may discover that we have forgotten the original question.

When we get lost, we need to have routine procedures in place to help us find our way. Knowing something about the terrain and its boundaries can help. When Dwight and I hike in the forest behind our mountain cabin, we have some guidelines to help us find our way: Follow the ridges up to the high points where you can get your bearings; take the valleys down until they intersect a stream, then go downstream until you reach a road. Following these suggestions helps us in familiar territory, but they wouldn't work in a roadless wilderness area!

Anywhere we find ourselves, however, we need to avoid certain actions. Frenetic searching without thinking ahead or without paying attention to where we have been only makes matters worse. We need to pay attention to clues that help us keep our sense of direction. Sometimes we need to find a visible location and stay put so that others can find us. We must be miserly with sources of nutrition and water unless and until we can replenish our supply.

Communities of faith also go through seasons of searching. They become unsure of their mission, uncertain about their identity, unclear about their calling. Neither frenetic activity nor sitting down to wait for a revelation seems to help. They question whether what happens to them is due to the Lord's work or their own.

Another biblical image that applies here is what the disciples experienced after the Resurrection and before Pentecost. We read that "when they had entered the city, they went to the room upstairs where they were staying. . . . All these were constantly devoting themselves to prayer" (Acts 13a, 14a). To the early Christians, it might have seemed like nothing much was happening. They were just continuing with their usual practice of prayer. But all the time, something profound was taking place, and without prayer they would have been unprepared for the gift of the Spirit on Pentecost. We believe the Holy Spirit was working with them all along.

Searching is a sacramental process, and we need to stay focused on the object of our search. But if we concentrate only on what we want to find, we will surely miss amazing sights along the way. The waterfall we didn't know was there, the largest squirrel's "kitchen" we have ever seen, the magnificent carpet of moss on a beautiful granite boulder— these are just a few of the blessings we have experienced while exploring the beautiful, forested mountains in the Black Hills of South Dakota.

We need to learn to keep heading toward our goal and at the same time attend to the little blessings along the way. Sacramental searching is like that. We find that the process itself serves as a channel of God's grace. While we are looking for something else, God has a way of blessing us with gifts we did not expect, a teaching we weren't aware we needed, or nourishment from an unexpected source.

We seldom think of our mundane meanderings as sacramental; we wouldn't consider them so mundane if we did! Still, there is deep truth in the fact that the early Christians were described as "followers of the Way" (Acts 9:2, GNT.) Christians are not people who have arrived but people "on the way," so the journey itself must be *sign*-ificant. The Way becomes sacramental for us when we recognize Christ in the stranger who walks beside us and know that God walks with us. God's presence does not depend upon our recognizing this presence. But when awareness of God breaks in upon us, that which appears to be mundane meandering becomes sacramental. In the nineteenth century, John Mason Neale used these words to translate the affirmations of the eighth-century saint, Stephen of Mar Saba:

> Finding, following, keeping, struggling,
> Is he sure to bless?
> Saints, apostles, prophets, martyrs,
> Answer, Yes.[10]

Whether in our everyday ordinary, our wilderness wanderings, or our seasons of searching, looking at the mundane through the lens of the sacramental enables us to know these words are true for ordinary people like us. When we open our hearts to the Spirit and our eyes to the world around us, God's grace gives the song we are living both purpose and hope.

# Notes

1. Gabe Huck, *How Can I Keep from Singing?*: *Thoughts about Liturgy for Musicians* (Chicago: Liturgy Training Publications, 1989), 27.

2. Ernesto Cardenal, *Abide in Love* (Maryknoll, N.Y.: Orbis Books, 1995), 33.

3. Sue Bender, *Everyday Sacred: A Woman's Journey Home* (San Francisco: HarperSanFrancisco, 1995), ix.

4. Ibid., 158–59.

5. Ibid., 47.

6. Our friend Ellen Oliver taught us that there is no such thing as a coincidence. She says, "Call it what it is—a 'God-incidence!'"

7. Quoted by Leonard Healy, "The Burren: Not At All Barren," in *Ireland of the Welcomes* 50:1 (January–February 2001): 14.

8. Ruth Duck's hymn, "Lead On, O Cloud of Presence," uses this phrase. See *The Faith We Sing* (Nashville, Tenn.: Abingdon Press, 2000), No. 2234.

9. From stanzas 2–3 of "How Firm a Foundation," *The United Methodist Hymnal* (Nashville, Tenn.: The United Methodist Publishing House, 1989), No. 529.

10. Final stanza of "Art Thou Weary, Art Thou Languid" found in *The Book of Hymns* (Nashville, Tenn.: The United Methodist Publishing House, 1966), No. 99.

# Disruptive Discords

*Although it is made of thin, delicate strands, the web is not easily broken. However, a web gets torn everyday by the insects that kick around in it, and a spider must rebuild it when it gets full of holes.*

—E. B. White
*Charlotte's Web*

We met our friends Taylor and June McConnell for the Palm Sunday service at St. John's United Methodist Church in Santa Fe. They said, "We are going to a service of solidarity at St. Bede's Episcopal Church this afternoon. Would you like to go?"

St. Bede's, a small congregation, meets in an octagonal sanctuary with glass windows looking out on the high desert landscape. During the previous six weeks vandals had struck the church six times, smashing the windows at first with baseball bats and finally with an ax. The church could no longer view the destruction as random. In spite of their spending money on an alarm system and increased surveillance, the perpetrators had not been caught. The congregation's insurance deductible rose from $250 to $2500 per incident. They felt vulnerable and were in shock.

St. Bede's is an inclusive congregation that sees itself as "a Christ-centered servant community rooted in biblical teaching and Christian tradition as practiced by the Episcopal Church." We found it to be racially inclusive, welcoming "traditional and nontraditional households" into its faith family.[1] A rainbow flag flies outside the church as a sign of welcome to all of God's children. As we gathered that Palm Sunday afternoon, we had to park on a neighboring street. Walking by several state and local police cars, we joined over 500 others from many different denominations and faiths in a sanctuary that seats 250. Linda sat in an aisle on the floor. Someone behind her said, "I hope the fire marshal isn't here!" Another person quipped, "Well, there are plenty of windows, and we know they break!"

Not an inch of standing or sitting room remained, and more than 170 persons stood outside open windows where they could hear and see, sing and pray with us. Rabbis, priests, pastors of many different congregations, and representatives from the council of churches and from organizations representing gay and lesbian Christians and the NAACP spoke and led in prayers. Choirs from three different faith communities sang. Representatives of two Presbyterian youth groups led the congregation in a pledge of nonviolence. We shared laughter and tears.

After the service we joined others in the fellowship hall and outside the church walls as folks shared food (donated by a local food store) and received thanks from many St. Bede's members who were overwhelmed by the outpouring of support from so many. Some Los Alamos residents said, "We came because you were there for us last summer during the fire."

The everyday ordinary with its times of wandering and

searching is broken by disruptive discords that disturb us. They interrupt the flow of the expected, the appropriate, what seems right and fitting. Bad things do happen to good people, and these catastrophes feel out of proportion to what we feel anyone deserves. Such difficult times offend our sense of justice. Deep within us rises the childhood cry, "It isn't fair!"

A loyal and diligent employee comes to work one day and finds he no longer has a job. A spouse answers the door and receives a legal document that says the marriage is ending. The phone rings in the middle of the night, and parents learn that their son or daughter is in jail. A congregation comes to worship and discovers that their new pastor, whom they already greatly love, is leaving. Children are told they will have to leave their friends because the family is moving.

None of these situations occurs by choice. We don't desire such occasions, but they happen. Into the steady pattern of life, discords jar us with their unpleasant, unwanted, unexpected realities.

Yet even in situations like these, life goes on. It faces us with the rude question, "So what are you going to do about it?" We can't change what has happened, as much as we would like to. Grief overwhelms us.

Our responses vary. Often our first reaction is denial: "There must be some mistake. It can't be true." We may be angry: "How could they!" We may be vindictive: "Just wait; they'll be sorry." We may be cynical: "Well, what did you expect? That's life." Or we may even be apathetic or depressed: "Nothing I do makes any difference anyway.

Who cares?" More than likely, we will move through all these responses and similar ones—slowly or quickly, consciously or unconsciously. Grief is real and must be reckoned with as we move beyond the initial shock of what has happened. And whatever our responses, we are vulnerable.

Tensions arise with others who experience the same disruptive discord because each individual responds to trials differently. When we are trying to cope with crisis in our own way, we become annoyed when someone tells us "Every cloud has a silver lining—wait and see"; or "When life hands you lemons, make lemonade"; or "When the going gets tough, the tough get going." Such pieces of folk wisdom have their place, but during a crisis they seem fake, out of touch with reality, and unhelpful. Nothing is less helpful than to tell a depressed or angry person not to feel that way. Our feelings aren't good or bad—they just *are*. What we do with them can be good or bad, but feelings must be lived through.

Perhaps the most disturbing response comes from persons who see the hand of God in our troubles and imply that God must be punishing us for a sin, is testing our faith, or knows we are strong and can take it. The image of God revealed in such comments as these deeply troubles us. (We've all known people like Job's "friends," and we wish they would go away!) Surely this is not the God revealed to us in Jesus Christ.

Yet such perspectives contain a grain of truth. Our faith is tested. Past words and actions do come back to haunt us. To view God as the cause of our trials, however, leads us in the wrong direction. To invest our troubles with the mistaken notion that they are "God's will" adds insult to injury. What kind of a loving God would cause catastrophe, even to wayward children? That would be bad news, indeed.

Consider the experience of two Andover-Newton seminary students whose young child had just died of leukemia. When they opened their door, there stood their beloved professor, noted theologian Nels F. S. Ferré. He opened his arms to them both. As he embraced them with tears streaming down his face, he said, "God is crying too."

During disruptive discords we can look to the good news: God is Emmanuel, God-with-us. God is not absent, even from the cross. Sometimes in the midst of our troubles, we receive as grace the assurance that God is with us in spite of our troubles, and we give thanks. The knowledge that God is with us sustains and strengthens us.

What can we do when that assurance is absent? We can remember that God is present regardless of whether we *feel* God's presence. Even when our prayers seem to bounce off the ceiling, God hears. Even when the feeling of God's absence seems overwhelming, God is still Emmanuel. Faith means acting on that assurance even when we don't feel it, praying when we don't think God is listening, daring to "go through the motions" of faith when we don't feel like people of faith.

Trials don't last forever. Often our troubles aren't a matter of life and death, even though they seem that way. Gradually we recover our perspective. We recognize that situations could be worse, that hope is present even in the midst of tribulation, that God's grace suffices.

## Pondering Paradox

Paradox didn't receive too much attention in a world where rational discourse and logic were dominant. Many now recognize, however, that we ignore paradox to our detriment. Paradox is built into the whole of creation. Huge ocean waves can be majestic and destructive. Chemotherapy can both save lives and result in horrible, life-threatening side effects. We can love our children deeply and still be terribly angry with them.

Harvey Cox tackles two seemingly paradoxical verses from John's Gospel. In John 14:2, Jesus assures his disciples, "In my Father's house there are many dwelling places." He then responds to Thomas's question about how they will know the way to where Jesus is going by telling him, "I am the way, and the truth, and the life. No one comes to the Father except through me" (v. 6). Cox says, "From Jesus I have learned both that he is the Way and that in God's house there are many mansions. I do not believe these two sayings are contradictory. In fact I have come to see that only by understanding one can we come to understand the other."[2]

When we can live with paradox, we do not need to ask which statement is true. In fact, we become free to ask a different question: "What is God's truth for me in each of these assertions by Jesus?"

Paradox allows us to hold seemingly contradictory claims or assumptions at the same time. We believe that our denomination (United Methodists), like many others, seeks to be a faithful member of the body of Christ. We also believe that some of our denomination's stances conflict with the gospel. We must attend to both of these beliefs if we are to be faithful disciples of Jesus Christ. How can we do this?

If we did not believe that our denomination is the best institutional expression and embodiment of the gospel in our time, we would need to find a better one. But we are committed to Jesus Christ and believe that John Wesley's theology of prevenient (before we are aware), justifying (saving), and sanctifying (going on to perfection) grace is a powerful way to acknowledge and appropriate God's grace for all. We believe that testing our decisions by scripture, tradition, (Christian) experience, and reason (the Wesleyan quadrilateral) gives us the best possible guide for discerning and deciding how to act as faithful disciples. We affirm most of the ecumenical and social principles of The United Methodist Church. It is our church—imperfect but "going on to perfection"!

We believe that God calls the church to show inclusive love and openness to all God's children. We grieve over the pain our denomination's stance has caused for gay and lesbian Christians and their families in our congregation, in many churches, and in our nation and world. But we remain United Methodists because we believe that God's inclusive love will prevail and that God calls us to witness and work toward that end.

As we told persons preparing to join the congregations we pastored, "If you agree with 90 percent of the church's social principles, beliefs, and practices, this is probably the right denomination for you. If you disagree with many of them, you might want to think more about your decision."

Denominations, as well as individual Christians, are going on to perfection, and we will never fully reach perfection this side of Christ's return. Every Christian is called to be open to prophetic calls to help us perfect our stands for social justice, our worship and study life together, and our witness in the world.

Learning to live with paradox is often difficult. The presence of paradox is no excuse for avoiding hard intellectual work. It does not mean we can sail through life with the attitude *It doesn't matter what you believe, as long as you believe it sincerely.* What we believe *does* matter. And what we do matters even more!

Another paradox comes into play here. We are called to love and accept and go to the Lord's Table with Christians who believe differently than we do. We may disagree about styles of music or worship or infant baptism or homosexuality. But one measure of faithfulness is whether we can be humble enough to accept that we *all* see through a glass dimly. Christians are called to bring about what we understand to be the gospel, without resorting to methods that no one can defend as consistent with Christ's life or teachings.

## Wrestling

Sometimes we are caught between a rock and a hard place. Life-and-death decisions confront us, but we are uncertain about which way leads to life and which to death.

Jacob had cheated his brother, Esau, out of his birthright and blessing and fled to live with his uncle Laban. (See Genesis 27–32 for the entire story.) Laban comes to believe

Jacob has cheated him, and Jacob, in an attempt to escape him, heads for home. With Laban behind him and Esau coming to meet him, Jacob is in a difficult position.

Jacob sends presents to Esau, then sends his servants, wives, and children ahead with all his possessions, but he stays behind. We read in Genesis 32:24 that "a man wrestled with him until daybreak." Even though his hip is dislocated, Jacob won't let go of his antagonist until he receives a blessing. Then suddenly the names in the story change. Jacob receives a new name, Israel (literally, "one who strives with God"), for he has "striven with God and with humans, and . . . prevailed." Jacob names the place where he wrestled with God "Peniel" (literally, "the face of God"), "for I have seen God face to face, and yet my life is preserved" (v. 30). He is left with a new name and a limp.

Recognizing the truth behind this strange account is not hard: Jacob has no easy options. He can't go back to Laban; he is afraid to go forward to Esau. Danger lies in both directions. The situation is a matter of life and death. So he wrestles. At first it seems like human wrestling, agonizing over a decision. But Jacob won't let go. He won't surrender to the belief that "whatever will be, will be." He hangs on, and when the blessing comes, he understands that he has wrestled with God. He is no longer who he was. He has a new name . . . and a limp.

When the disruptive discords of life confront us, sometimes we find ourselves wrestling with decisions that have life-changing implications. They are not easy choices; the right road is not distinctly marked. We cannot know all the consequences of our choices and how things will turn out if we choose this instead of that. But as we grapple with who we are and what we are called to do, we become aware that God is with us. We can no longer be the same. Something about our identity has changed; we know who we are in relation to God in a new way. But we also have a limp that will be a part of us from now on. The battle has marked us, and every step we take from here on out will bear witness to that wrestling.

Choosing between what are clearly good and evil alternatives may not be difficult for us. If we have chosen to be on God's side, that earlier decision will determine what we see as best for us now. On the other hand, if we have already succumbed to the power of evil so that patterns of hate or lust or greed have become deeply ingrained in our nature, continuing to walk that road will be easier.

At times, however, the choices aren't nearly as clear-cut. We may have to choose between schools to attend, between values that seem equally important, between patterns of behavior in which we have tried to "have our cake and eat it too," between people, between political loyalties, between strategies, between jobs. Whichever way we go, we will have to give up what is part of the other path. We are left with a "limp" to mark our encounter.

Often we can't recognize which option will allow us to remain faithful to our calls. We faced a time like this when Linda was asked to apply for a teaching position at Garrett-Evangelical. She resisted. We struggled. We had only been at St. Luke's for two years, and God was blessing our ministry there. We enjoyed ministering as a team. It was a time of painful discernment. We believed that God honored our marriage vows as we do. If Linda was being called to a new place, what about Dwight's call? How were we to know the right decision? What would it mean for each of us and both of us to be faithful?

We prayed. We sought the counsel of our district superintendent and our bishop—spiritual counsel to help us discern, not advice about what we should do. We tested our tentative scenarios with trusted Christian friends. Finally we made a decision and then were able to pray: "God, we do not know if we have discerned rightly, but we've done the best we know. If it is your will, bless our decisions and use them for your glory. If we have not seen clearly your way for us, use our decisions to your glory anyway and help get us back on track."

There is consolation in believing the good news of the gospel: that as long as we try to discern God's will, God can use our decisions for good. We don't have to struggle with, "But what if we make the wrong decision?" The good news of the gospel is that we do not have to be perfect for God to love and bless us. As long as we seek openness to the Holy Spirit, God will walk with us on the paths we choose.

Sometimes those times of wrestling come early in life, sometimes late. Sometimes they seem to be our almost constant companions. Just after his baptism, Jesus wrestled with temptations. (See Matthew 4:1-11; Mark 1:12-13; and Luke 4:1-13.) His response to his temptations implied how he would live out the ministry and mission to which he was called. Indeed, as Matthew 4:1 records, he was "led up by the Spirit" to face those alternatives. Mark 1:12 puts it even more forcefully: "And the Spirit immediately drove him out into the wilderness." We rarely choose times of wrestling, but our priorities and values are clarified through them. As a result of his temptations, Jesus came to know something about the goals and strategies of his ministry. To look an option in the eye and say "No! That is not who I am and what I am about" can be grace for us. To say "yes," even though it meant living apart with a commuter marriage for a time, was scary for us. But once we discerned this option as our calling, God blessed our yes (even with its year apart).

During that year apart (which we didn't like any better than we thought we would!), we wrestled with what we should do. Every door we tried to open seemed to close in our faces. One day as Dwight read the story of Saul's conversion in Acts 9, words he had never noticed before jumped off the page at him: "Get up and enter the city, and you will be told what you are to do" (v. 6). With an inner assurance that those words were a sign of the Spirit's prompting, the blessing came; the decision to move to Chicago seemed the right way to go.

But Dwight was left with a limp: leaving a pastorate he loved and work he still misses, going where he had no job and no assurance of one. The situation did not work out quickly. Difficult years with many part-time jobs followed. But one opportunity after another began to open up for him at the seminary. Now we are both in ministry as we teach and learn with students at Garrett-Evangelical.

Rarely do such times of wrestling spell the end of the confrontation, even though they are decisive events. At the end of the temptation story, Luke writes that the devil "departed from [Jesus] until an opportune time" (4:13). Those opportune times just keep coming for us, as they did for Jesus. We always seem to have opportunities to turn our backs on the priorities we chose during our wrestling times.

Even more troubling, sometimes God leads us to see that we have misunderstood the nature of the values we have chosen. When Dwight answered the call to ministry, he thought his call meant being the pastor of a local church. When his college president, Harry Kalas, invited him to prepare for a teaching career, Dwight thought he had his priorities straight, so he said, "No, I'm called to the ministry." Dr. Kalas replied, "That's what I'm talking about." Coming to recognize teaching as his sphere of ministry, Dwight had to readjust again when he received the call to become pastor of St. Luke's United Methodist Church in Dubuque and yet again when he joined the faculty at Garrett-Evangelical Theological Seminary. Gradually Dwight has come to realize that the "call to ministry" concerns *how* he teaches or pastors rather than where. In baptism all Christians are marked for ministry. For some, ordination takes place within the circle of that ministry. Wrestling with the nature of our ministry keeps reemerging, and the basic decision to answer God's call is a decisive factor in everything that follows. But our calls as baptized Christians may lead us to surprising and unimaginable places!

Jesus had to wrestle with his mission again in the garden of Gethsemane. (See Mark 14:32-42.) He prayed that the cup of suffering and death might be taken from him. He had been faithful. He had preached, healed, taught, and acted. Why couldn't he just slip away and live a quiet life out in the desert? What good would result from his death? His disciples didn't seem to "get it" yet. Couldn't he take them out to a lonely place where they could pray and learn together? They weren't likely to change the power of Rome or the hearts of the religious authorities. Since Jesus was fully human, such questions must have flooded his mind. How disheartening it must have been at this time of deep struggle and wrestling to return to his disciples and find them asleep instead of watching and praying through this struggle with him.

Yet the conclusion of his prayer is clear: "Not my will but yours be done." The decision was not easy. We read that "in his anguish he prayed more earnestly, and his sweat became like great drops of blood falling down on the ground" (Luke 22:42-44). He did not seek death, but he did not flee from it. He confronted the religious and secular authorities. They could not accept his mission and ministry, so they killed him.

Jesus' death caused his disciples a disruptive discord of monumental proportions. On the road to Emmaus one of them confessed to the stranger: "We had hoped that he was the one to redeem Israel" (Luke 24:21). That hope had died with Jesus' crucifixion. The disciples wrestled with its implications and could not shrug it off. Deep loss and anguished wrestling walked down the Emmaus road together. The stranger reminded the two disciples of their faith heritage. Only later could they say: "Were not our hearts burning within us while he was talking to us on the road, while he was opening the scriptures to us?" (24:32). Signs of grace are often invisible at the moment; only in retrospect can we see them at all. But disruptive discords are part of the times and seasons of our lives. We dare not pretend they are not part of us.

## Deep Loss

Sometimes the disruptive discord is a matter of life and death. On January 5, 1991, our dear friends Mary and Jim Purdy received a phone call that changed their lives forever. Their eighteen-year-old daughter, who was living in Spain as a Rotary exchange student, had been killed in an accident.[3]

For over a week, the Purdy family and their faith community waited for Jenny's body to arrive from Spain. Her brother arrived home from Guatemala, where he was serving in the Peace Corps, and still they waited. On Sunday, January 13, her uncle spoke briefly to the congregation. He thanked them for fulfilling the vows they took at Jenny's baptism, for St. Luke's United Methodist Church had nurtured her in faith and in a love for God that was deep and real. "Tomorrow," he said, "she will again be beside this font as her casket is placed here. And with breaking hearts, together we will give her back to God."

On that first Good Friday, the disciples ran away from the cross where the one they had believed would save Israel hung dying. Jesus' mother and several other women who knew and loved Jesus remained there watching Jesus die on that despicable cross—perhaps frozen in their grief and sense of loss.

At times like these, we feel as though there can be no future. The loss of a beloved child leaves little room for hope. With a child's death, dreams die. What might have been can be no more. Death has snatched this person from our presence, and we know life will never be the same again. Grief and anguish overwhelm us.

Mary clung to me after her daughter's funeral and said, "Linda, how can I go on?" That is the same question those two disciples were struggling with on the third day after the crucifixion as they walked those seven long miles home from Jerusalem to Emmaus. (See Luke 24:13-35.)

But Jesus appeared to them that day and helped them see in a new way. He listened to them and reminded them of what the scriptures say about the Messiah. Still they did not recognize him. When they arrived home he appeared to be traveling further, but they invited him to stay with them and have dinner. Finally, as Jesus—whom they still saw only as that stranger who walked with them on the road— took bread, blessed, and broke it, they recognized who he was. He disappeared from their sight, but now they *knew!* Tired though they must have been, they could do nothing but hurry those seven miles back to Jerusalem to tell the other disciples that Jesus lived.

Death did not have the last word, for Jesus lives! The vision of God's kin-dom[4] of justice and compassion lives! Death cannot overcome it! And because Jesus lives, Jim and Mary and St. Luke's can affirm that Jenny also lives. She lives with Jesus and the communion of all the saints. Though their hearts are breaking and anger still burns in their chests, there is that faint, flickering realization that death will never have the last word. We can go on in the face of all the disruptions that confront us because we know that God weeps with us, God never stops loving us, and that no matter what happens, God finally wins and embraces us in that victory!

The most traumatic family disruption Dwight and I have ever experienced came in a phone call we received at church in the Black Hills. We were singing the first hymn on June 18, 1978, when the pastor came out of the chancel to hand us a note asking us to call friends in Topeka, Kansas. We guessed they were planning to come for a visit. Since they knew we didn't have a phone at the cabin, they called us at church.

After church, we returned the call. What a shock! Our friends had just heard on the news that the night before, a small showboat, the *Whippoorwill*, had capsized on Lake Pomona in Kansas when a freak tornado struck. Dwight's Aunt Grace and Uncle Milton and their son and daughter and two grandchildren were aboard—celebrating Aunt Grace's retirement and their fortieth wedding anniversary. Aunt Grace; their daughter, Sandra; and her daughter, Melissa, had drowned. Melissa's body had not yet been recovered. At a family celebration, in the twinkling of an eye, women from three generations of our family were gone.

Later that month Dwight reflected on this experience and wrote in his weekly newspaper column:

> Within that tragic battered home, one perspective penetrated all the planning and grieving and remembering and consoling. Early in the week someone said to my uncle, "I don't see how you can go on." "There isn't any alternative," he replied. "All my ministry I've told others that God is good. God loves and cares. God's grace is sufficient for every need. Now I know there is nothing else on which we can rely."[5]

During the remaining years of his life, though his health never fully returned from the trauma of nearly drowning and losing his wife, daughter, and granddaughter, Uncle Milton embodied his belief that God's grace is sufficient. He worked with grief and loss groups, continued to preach when pastors were gone, and came to see us when he could. We were able to share our beloved Black Hills with him before he died.

Though the web of life is fragile, God's grace is sufficient for those who trust in God. No matter what disruptions come, God and the church—the body of Christ—sustain us and see us through. Through tears, depression, and despair, we acknowledge that God does not forsake those who will receive the costly love that is freely offered. As we learned from the tragedy of the *Whippoorwill*, even times of deep loss can become a sacramental season when we allow the mystery of God's gracious presence to grasp us.

# *Notes*

1. Quoted from an information card found in the pew rack and on a table inside the front door.
2. Harvey Cox, *Many Mansions: A Christian's Encounter with Other Faiths* (Boston, Mass.: Beacon Press, 1988), 19.
3. For an account of how this family and their faith community dealt with Jenny's death, see Linda J. Vogel, *Rituals for Resurrection: Celebrating Life and Death* (Nashville, Tenn.: Upper Room Books, 1996).
4. We prefer the term *kin-dom* to *kingdom* because the former emphasizes the family of God.
5. "Dwight Vogel's Perspective," *LeMars Daily Sentinel* (LeMars, Iowa), 30 June 1978, 4.

# Revealing Resurrections

*In the Spirit-giving resurrected Christ we find that the mystery,*
*the wonder, the suffering and the glory are one. He stands as*
*humanity's future, saying, "Behold, I make all things new."*
—Don E. Saliers
*Worship and Spirituality*

Faced with Jenny's tragic death, what enabled her family and the St. Luke's congregation to affirm God's love? How could Uncle Milton claim that "God's grace is sufficient" after his wife, daughter, and granddaughter drowned and he nearly did so himself? How could we dare to affirm that death did not have the last word? When disruptive discords enter our lives, what enables us to go on?

As we wrote and revised the last chapter on disruptive discords, we recognized that we kept spilling over into the focus of this chapter. Our attempts to postpone references to Resurrection dynamics until now stubbornly refused to make sense to us. We had to accept that for Christians, in ways we will make explicit later in this book, death and resurrection are indissolubly linked.

We believe that moments of mystery intersect both our seasons of mundane meandering and our times of despair and deep loss. We can never totally uncover the vast matrix of meanings that penetrates the fabric of our lives. To assume that we can unravel that vast tapestry and make logical sense of it is sheer folly. Life is deeper than logic, more than propositions that can be tested by sensory experiences. Yet our minds are part of who we are, and we have a relentless drive to decipher meaning from the seemingly random patterns that surround us. Mystery pervades life, and we are part of that mystery.

There is a cheap use of the word *mystery* that is not at all helpful. Rather than wrestling with meaning or opening ourselves to participation in deep mystery, we may be tempted to say, "It's just a mystery to me." When we say this, we mean, "I don't want to think about this situation any more."

*Mystery*, as we are using the word, is not an escape hatch for the mind. Nor is it a word for a puzzle that can be solved if only we can gather enough clues, as in a mystery novel. No, we are talking about a quality beyond our comprehension that is nonetheless real, impinging on our lives and apprehending us in unmistakable ways. When those moments of mystery come, it seems as though a veil is torn and we can see beyond what we can understand. Mystery is always more than we can understand, but it enables us to "know" in ways that are impossible without it. Mystery invites us to connect mind and spirit—with feelings as well as words and ideas. Encountering mystery requires us to let go of the illusion that we are in control.

For too long we have assumed that meaning is a rational act, the work of the mind on the basis of sensory observation and logical analysis. Thinking is important and essential to our being human. What has meaning for us, however, is deeper than what we think.

Recognizing mystery is more than just a rational act. It involves our minds, our emotions, our bodies. Mystery gives life meaning that is deeper than our minds can formulate. In mystery, we learn to live as whole beings.

We have a summer cabin in the mountains of western South Dakota. Every morning we go out on the front deck to greet the new day and to let the new day greet us. "Good morning, Morning," Linda says. It is an everyday, ordinary kind of experience. Sometimes morning mist rises from the mountain stream across the road and gradually vanishes in the sunlight.

One morning, it seemed as though a cloud had gone to sleep in our valley. The mist was thick, shrouding the mountaintops. The air was still. The scene was incredibly beautiful, a moment of mystery that grasped us.

We could make this particular morning an object lesson of life's meaning, such as, "There is more to life than can be seen," or "Just because we can't see them doesn't mean that the mountains aren't still there." But that wasn't our experience that morning. We were just present in that incredible beauty. It was more than us, yet we were part of it. It wrapped itself around us and included us, just as it included the rocks and trees and stream. We did not ask, "What does this moment mean?" We still cannot tell you its meaning in propositional language. Linda said it felt like we had stepped into a Monet painting. What we can tell you is this: We treasure that morning as an unforgettable moment of mystery. We live out of the meaning it has for us.

Those two disciples on the road to Emmaus experienced mystery too. Jesus had been crucified. Their hope was dead. The stranger opened to them scriptures they already knew, but they weren't able to connect this act with the one who spoke to them. Then when he blessed and broke the bread, they experienced the presence of Jesus! They recognized the stranger. Listen to what they said: "Were not our hearts burning within us while he was talking to us on the road?"(Luke 24:32). Taken at face value, these words alone—apart from the story, apart from our own experience of moments of mystery—are a strange, incomprehensible, logically impossible combination of words. Yet we know what they mean. The image of something so real and so deep within us that we can talk about our hearts burning within us makes sense to us, even though our senses cannot validate it. No wonder John Wesley could say that he felt his heart "strangely warmed"!

In a season of deep loss, those of us at Jennifer Purdy's funeral were also grasped by a moment of mystery. The question "Why, God, why?" did not go away, nor did our grief and distress diminish. But somehow in this community of God's people gathered to share their sense of loss, we found in the presence of one another, in music, in scripture, in witness by word and action a mystery: God was with us, and in God death does not have the last word. Our grief was touched by hugs and tears. The presence of others let us know we were not alone; our community would not let us sink irretrievably into the pain that sought to undo us. Our awareness of the presence of the living God even in the presence of death made this a sacramental time.

The community of Santa Maria de la Paz in Santa Fe has built a church filled with the work of local artists and artisans. Near the Lord's Table stands a large cross. Each arm of the cross has a slit in the middle so that one can see through it. The congregation understands the open configuration of that monumental cross as a symbol of resurrection. For them, it is "a passageway which allows us to move through and beyond the mystery of the passion."[1]

Recognition of mystery does not mean that we ignore the disruptive discords or trivialize the everyday ordinary. Moments of mystery take place within those very times and seasons, grasping us in ways beyond our understanding. How can we begin to embody revealing resurrection times so we can live into and out of their mystery?

## Mountaintop Experiences

Often mountaintop experiences are full of mystery. We can't get our minds around them, yet they provide meaning for our lives. Some important stories in the Bible have a mountaintop as their setting.

Moses received the Ten Commandments on Mount Sinai. We read in Deuteronomy:

> These words the LORD spoke with a loud voice to your whole assembly at the mountain, out of the fire, the cloud, and the thick darkness, and he added no more. He wrote them on two stone tablets, and gave them to me. When you heard the voice out of the darkness, while the mountain was burning with fire, you approached me, all the heads of your tribes and your elders; and you said, "Look, the LORD our God has shown us his glory and greatness, and we have heard his voice out of the fire." (5:22-24a)

Theater groups or movie producers who try to stage this scene push their creative and technological skills to the limit. This mountaintop experience is extremely spectacular.

Not all mountaintop experiences are spectacular, however. When Elijah met God at Mount Horeb, the mood was quite different:

> Now there was a great wind, so strong that it was splitting mountains and breaking rocks in pieces before the LORD, but the LORD was not in the wind; and after the wind an earthquake, but the LORD was not in the earthquake; and after the earthquake a fire, but the LORD was not in the fire; and after the fire a sound of sheer silence. When Elijah heard it, he wrapped his face in his mantle and went out and stood at the entrance of the cave. Then there came a voice to him that said, "What are you doing here, Elijah?" (1 Kings 19:11-13)

Two very different mountaintop experiences, yet in both of them God's presence is made known. Let's look at one more story, this time from the Gospels. In it we learn that "Jesus took with him Peter and James and John, and led them up a high mountain apart, by themselves." There Jesus "was transfigured before them, and his clothes became dazzling white, such as no one on earth could bleach them. And there appeared to them Elijah with Moses, who were talking with Jesus" (Mark 9:2-4).

Events in the Judeo-Christian tradition may be the genesis of our expression "mountaintop experiences." We know what the phrase means, even though what we call mountaintop experiences don't always happen on mountaintops. Sometimes these experiences come in a still small voice or even in sheer silence.

Whenever we find ourselves in the presence of mystery and the Spirit of God, we can say it was a mountaintop experience. Linda had such an encounter with the living God in the Canadian Rockies. It was a hard time for us because we were watching her dad die little by little from a brain tumor. One evening as we headed back to our campsite, we put Peter and Kris down to sleep in the back of our Volkswagen camper. As we drove along a curving mountain highway toward our campsite, Dwight downshifted. The door hadn't latched properly, and we heard our two-year-old say, "Pete gone! Pete bye-bye." As we frantically turned and drove back around a curve, Linda found Peter in the arms of a woman standing beside the road. As Linda took him in her own arms, she saw the fiery red sun disappear behind a mountain peak. Somehow in that moment, she realized that God gives life and God takes life. Peter lives. Her dad is dying. The gift of life comes undeserved and full of wonder. We can't figure it out; we can only receive it as God's grace. Linda's struggle to deal with her dad's dying vanished. In its place came an ability to trust God to be with us in that process. Guilt and anger evaporated. The unanswerable questions no longer weighed her down. Seeing her dad suffer still pained her, but in that moment, a kind of peace that can only be a gift settled over her.[2]

At times we seem more open to experiencing God's presence in high places, because awe wells up in us when we find our tiny selves in the presence of majestic peaks. But God touches and embraces us, challenging us in every kind of place and time. God's call and God's grace come. Sometimes they remain hidden and unreceived because we do not have ears to hear and eyes to see. Occasionally we see but turn our backs on the offered gift.

Our task is to accept the gifts God offers, to receive them gratefully. Jesus received with gratitude the gift offered by the woman at Bethany—her anointing with tears and expensive oil. (See Mark 14:3-9; Matthew 26:6-13; John 12:1-8.) Sometimes we are like the disciples who scolded and judged the woman for wasting resources that could feed the poor. We too may become so obsessed with our own priorities that we cannot receive the extravagant gifts God offers us.

When we close our eyes and open ourselves to remembering our mountaintop experiences, we find ourselves holding our beautiful daughter in our arms for the very first time; we find ourselves in the sanctuary at Calvary Church in LeMars at our children's confirmations; and at the little frame church in Martelle on Christmas Eve; and at St. Luke's in Dubuque early in the morning when the sun lights up those beautiful Tiffany windows. We remember sitting in our offices and being surprised by joy at the majestic organ music as Ruth Jones began practicing.

We feel the forest shrouded in mist as we stand on our deck in the Black Hills; we see and smell the festive mass celebrated by the monks at St. John's Abbey on All Saints' Eve; we go deep inside and relive the quiet conversation we shared with Sister Jeremy Hall in her hermitage and the blessing she gave us as we departed. We recall experiences of meeting God during chapel services at the seminary and while feeding homeless men at Epworth's shelter.

We taste the strong, hot tea shared with good friends in

Belfast. We relive walks on forest paths in the fall with leaves crackling under our feet, and seeing the first crocus in spring. We reexperience painful and joyous moments with our students when we recognized the Spirit in our midst.

We can still see the deep wrinkles and penetrating eyes of Mother Teresa as she talked with us in Calcutta, and we remember the eyes of the begging children outside. We hear again conversations about vocation, faith, and hope with Father David Fleming, S.M.,[3] as we traveled together in Europe, India, and across the United States.

Going to a mountaintop does not guarantee a sacramental experience. Indeed, being awed by beauty or overwhelmed by silence may not be sacramental, even though we may value those experiences. We have said that when a time is sacramental *we recognize the sacred*. We become *aware of the presence of God*. The divine presence is *revealed* to us, but it is not immediately apparent—it is also *hidden*. We must be grasped by that which is beyond the obvious. Thus God's presence is a gift we *receive*. Yet we must be open to *perceiving* the gift offered to us. That *gift* calls for *response*; it lays claim upon us. Through it we are made new. It is a revealing resurrection time for us.

There is no place where God is not present! Yet we desperately need memorable times, mountaintop experiences, to remind us of that reality. When we have eyes to see and ears to hear, when we take time to focus on being instead of doing, we open ourselves to sensing the presence of the living, ever-creating God of justice and compassion.

Meeting God in these mountaintop experiences is not a goal in itself, nor is the mountaintop a place where we can decide to settle in and stay. Like Moses on Mount Sinai or Jesus, Peter, James, and John on the Mount of Transfiguration, we must head back into the valleys and storms of life. We can do so with renewed energy, power, and direction because of our encounters with God, but receiving these gifts requires that we get back to work—seeking the lost, feeding the hungry, touching the lonely, and working for justice and peace.

While the rhythms of our lives are syncopated with grace-filled moments like these, the steady beat of the life of the world calls us back to parent and teach, to worship and work. We are called to walk into the valleys where pain and loss and apathy and hopelessness beckon for a touch or a presence that grace-touched persons can give.

## Dancing on the Gravestones

We returned to St. Bede's in Santa Fe to participate in their celebration of the Easter Vigil on Saturday evening. Throughout the service no one referred to the vandalism and destruction of the previous weeks, nor even to the service of solidarity of the previous Sunday. Instead, a new fire was kindled; the Easter candle was carried into the darkened church; the scripture story of salvation was heard; we shared in the baptismal covenant; and we celebrated the Easter Eucharist. All of it, in word, symbolic action, symbol, and song, said over and over again: "Christ is risen! Christ is risen indeed!"

The message of the Resurrection is central to the Christian faith. We already acknowledged the impossibility of

confining that message to this chapter. It has interpene-
trated all that we attempted to say. Yet the Resurrection
often bewilders us. We still remember the first Easter at St.
Luke's, when a faithful parishioner said to Dwight, who was
teaching an adult Sunday school class: "You are talking like
you think this really happened." For many people the
strange stories of Jesus' resurrection reflect on an event that
couldn't possibly be true.

In that, we are not so different from the first disciples as
we may think. When the women told the disciples the story
of their experience at the tomb, "these words seemed to
them an idle tale, and they did not believe them" (Luke
24:11). Thomas is not the only one who doubted, so perhaps they understood why he said, "Unless I see the mark
of the nails in his hands, and put my finger in the mark of
the nails and my hand in his side, I will not believe" (John
20:25b). The accounts of the Resurrection in the four
Gospels indicate that the disciples couldn't find language
adequate to express their experience.

Laurence Hull Stookey notes that we have sought to
tame the significance of the Resurrection by turning it into
a resuscitation, that is, a continuation of the human life of
Jesus.[4] The Bible contains other stories of persons being
brought back to life—the raising of Lazarus (John 11) and
Jairus's daughter (Luke 8) among them. Yet we know we are
not referring to them when we speak of *the* Resurrection.
When medical science succeeds in restoring a person to
life, we don't assume that incident is a resurrection!

Stookey observes how the Gospel stories themselves
move back and forth between language that suggests the

risen Jesus was a corpse brought back to life (he walks to Emmaus, eats a fish, and invites Thomas to touch his wounds) and language that indicates the risen Jesus is a ghost—an otherworldly figure (he is unrecognized, passes through locked doors, and vanishes from sight). Stookey concludes, "Granted, we have to use human categories, because they are all we have. . . . But neither way of thinking can get at this new reality. The resurrection is beyond our usual categories. . . . [H]uman words and ideas simply are insufficient to deal with what we have experienced in the presence of the Risen One among us."[5]

What do we know? We know that the disciples who fled the garden of Gethsemane became courageous witnesses to Jesus and defied the very court that had condemned their master. We know that the first Christians began meeting early on the first day of the week—a day that was not part of their religious tradition and was inconvenient in terms of secular patterns because Sunday was a workday for them. They baptized new converts into the death and resurrection of Jesus. They broke bread in a holy meal that recalled both the death of Jesus and his living presence among them.

Something decisive must have happened to cause all that. None of the Gospel writers tries to describe the Resurrection itself; they only tell us the experiences of people as a result of the Resurrection. We aren't going to try to describe it either. The greatest witness to the Resurrection is the changed lives of people, the emergence of a dynamic community of faith.

Dwight remembers sitting in the Easter morning service at St. John's United Methodist Church in Santa Fe and realizing, *This isn't only about Jesus. Perhaps it isn't even primarily about Jesus. It is about the presence of Jesus in us. It's about new life in Jesus Christ.* And then he thought, *I've known that all my life, but I hadn't recognized what I knew. For as long as I can remember, one of my favorite Easter songs concludes, "You ask me how I know he lives? He lives within my heart."*[6]

But the Resurrection is more than that. The risen Christ lives in the community of faith begun by the first disciples and carried on by churches in many times and places ever since. *Resurrection* is the word we use for our incorporation into the mystery of Jesus Christ, our union with the one who was with God from the beginning and without whom nothing was made that was made (see John 1); who was crucified, died, was buried, and rose again on the third day; who is with us in the presence of the Holy Spirit; who is the First and Last, the Alpha and the Omega of creation and of human history.

Dwight's parents had planned carefully in advance for their passing. Whenever we were home, Dad would show us the metal file box containing all the vital papers, especially the file labeled "Funerals" with booklets for each funeral service. When Dad died, we went to that file and incorporated his requests into his funeral service. Dwight told Linda, "Put a copy of Dad's funeral bulletin in that file; we can use it as a guide when Mother's time comes."

We didn't know that within three weeks we would be opening that file box again. Alone after sixty-two years of marriage, Dwight's mother told Linda: "I just don't have anything left to fight with." And so, despite antibiotics flowing into both arms, pneumonia raced through her body. When we went to the funeral file, however, a surprise awaited. Tucked inside the planning booklet was a recipe card in Mother's writing, with the simple heading "Funeral." Bach's settings of three chorales were listed for the prelude, as was an organ meditation on "Near to the Heart of God." But the real gift was the listing of this scripture reference:

> He has rescued us from the power of darkness and transferred us into the kingdom of his beloved Son, in whom we have redemption, the forgiveness of sins.
>
> He is the image of the invisible God, the firstborn of all creation; for in him all things in heaven and on earth were created. . . . He himself is before all things, and in him all things hold together. He is the head of the body, the church; he is the beginning, the firstborn from the dead, so that he might come to have first place in everything. For in him all the fullness of God was pleased to dwell, and through him God was pleased to reconcile to himself all things, whether on earth or in heaven, by making peace through the blood of his cross. (Colossians 1:13-20)

Resurrection reveals to us who God is and who we are in God through Christ Jesus. Furthermore, it creates new life in us and constitutes a new community of which we are a part.

But it does not do this by pretending death does not exist. Without minimizing the deep loss death brings, Resurrection enables us to dance on the gravestones because we know death does not have the last word. The last word always belongs to God.

The church of Our Lady of Guadalupe at Villanueva, New Mexico, was locked, but the clerk of the general store across the road directed us to a house not far away. There we met Albert Garcia, whose family has lived in the valley for eleven generations. He said, "Stop at the cemetery. The first three rows of graves are all our family—from the last four hundred years!"

After showing us the house he was restoring, Garcia went with us to unlock the church, built in 1805. On the inside walls all around the church were folk-art fabric hangings embroidered by families of the parish, depicting the history of the Spanish in that valley and the life of that congregation across those four hundred years. One of the panels contained these embroidered words: "Since the entire earth is steeped in the grace of God, Christ's victory meets us at every step." That's what the Resurrection is all about. And that is why we can dare to dance on the gravestones of our lives.

## *Notes*

1. *Santa Maria de la Paz: Our Church, Its Images and Artists*—brochure from Santa Maria de la Paz community, Santa Fe, New Mexico.

2. See Dwight W. Vogel and Linda J. Vogel, *Sacramental Living: Falling Stars and Coloring Outside the Lines* (Nashville, Tenn.: Upper Room Books, 1999), 16–17 for a fuller account of this epiphany.

3. Father David Fleming is superior general of the Society of Mary (S.M.) and currently resides in Rome.

4. Laurence Hull Stookey, *Calendar: Christ's Time for the Church* (Nashville, Tenn.: Abingdon Press, 1996), 33–38.

5. Ibid., 36–37.

6. From "He Lives," words by Alfred H. Ackley, 1933, *The United Methodist Hymnal* (Nashville, Tenn.: The United Methodist Publishing House, 1989), No. 310.

# Sabbath Renewal

*Keeping Sabbath involves rhythm-breaking as well as falling
into God's rhythm and developing a new rhythm altogether.*
—Kenda Creasy Dean and Ron Foster
*The Godbearing Life*

In the everyday ordinary of the natural world, seasons of
growth are followed by seasons of rest and renewal. The two
of us have always lived in places with four seasons. In
spring, the trees begin to bud; flowers emerge from the soil;
and grasses turn green. Over the summer, plant life grows
and develops and bears fruit. When autumn comes, leaves
of the trees color and turn brown. Many fall from the trees
to nourish the soil. Frosts come, and most of the plants die
back. Winter brings a time of rest and renewal for roots,
bulbs, and seeds.

Indoor gardeners learn that they need to contrive that
period for some plants, putting them in a dark, cool place
for their "winter." Even areas with less contrasting seasons
experience patterns: rainy seasons and dry seasons; shifting
wind directions; times of blossoming, harvest, and renewal.

Our bodies also need renewal time. Hours of activity
and consciousness are followed by hours of sleep. When

traveling disturbs our sleep schedule, we have to readjust. Jet lag makes us aware of both our need for sleep and our need for regular patterns. While human beings seem to require different amounts of sleep (whether because of conditioning, body chemistry, or both), without sleep we can't function well. And when responsibilities, grief, anxiety, or stress makes sleeping difficult, we know that our future well-being depends upon being able to sleep.

Sometimes we think of sleep as a time when nothing happens, although we know better. Not only do our physical bodies continue operating during sleep (heart, lungs, digestion, regeneration are some examples), but our brains also stay active. Dreams and nightmares remind us of that fact. But even more activity occurs during sleep.

Many of us have gone to sleep working on a difficult problem and then awakened to find the solution. Musicians may practice a difficult passage one day with little success, only to return to it the next day to find that somehow the interaction between mind and fingers works much better. Our therapist believes that during sleep the brain is able to put things together in ways we can't during the session itself. She works with her clients to enable that to happen, and the results have been remarkable.

It isn't true that nothing happens during sleep or winter or times of apparent dormancy. Re-creative restoration takes place, and without it something goes dreadfully wrong with health and wholeness. Such patterns can teach us about our spiritual journeys. As individuals and congregations, we need sabbath times for rest and renewal. Such times involve breaking some of the ordinary rhythms by giving us the opportunity to become aware of God's rhythm. They can help us develop new rhythms that "keep sabbath" and open us to God's syncopated grace.

We have chosen to use the word *sabbath* to refer to such times and seasons. We begin by remembering that at the close of the sixth day of creation, God viewed the whole creation God had made and declared that "indeed, it was very good." Scripture tells us that on the seventh day, God rested. "So God blessed the seventh day and hallowed it." (See Genesis 1:31–2:3.)

God's blessing of the seventh day is why our Jewish brothers and sisters observe Sabbath from sundown Friday until sundown on Saturday. Into that religious pattern Christianity was born. But Christians began observing not the seventh day but the first day of the week as their holy day. They spoke of it as the Lord's Day because it was the day when the Resurrection occurred. As we have noted, for the early Christians, Sunday was a regular workday. Neither the Jewish community nor the Greco-Roman world saw the day as holy in any way. Thus Christians had to meet early in the morning or at night after work. Yet the drive for "sabbath time" was strong, and as the influence of Christianity increased, some Jewish understandings of the seventh-day "Sabbath" were transferred to "the Lord's Day" on Sunday.

The important point is that out of every seven days, human beings need to intentionally set apart time to re-creatively renew their connection with God, others, and themselves. Sabbath is a time to step out of routine and to set priorities straight.

For some of our ancestors in the faith, Sunday was a day

for worship and rest. Linda's grandmother lived with her family and strictly observed Sunday as "sabbath." She loved to play checkers but never would do so on Sunday. In her grade school years it seemed to Linda that her grandmother felt you couldn't do anything on Sunday but go to church and sit! Many communities still enforced "blue laws," so few businesses were open, and malls were a thing of the future. Dwight remembers family discussions about whether they should eat out on Sunday, since they were refraining from work but causing others to work to serve them.

For many persons in the twenty-first century, however, Sunday is just as busy as the other six days of the week. Christians may still squeeze in worship, but many congregations feel pressured to provide a "one-hour experience" where children can go to Sunday school while parents worship so that the whole family can move on to other activities. Children's sports leagues have usurped what seemed to them to be a slight opening in people's calendars so that now in some communities, sports and other activities are scheduled on Sunday mornings.

We know preschoolers who participate in gymnastics, swimming, cooking lessons, Spanish or French lessons, music lessons, ballet, T-ball, and on and on. Little time remains for them to play in the yard, lie on their back and watch the clouds, read a book, or take a nap. By the time children begin school, many families run themselves ragged transporting children here and there. Teenagers and parents have their own full schedules to keep.

Many, like us, know the value of sabbath rest but still find themselves captive to calendars that are full to overflowing. Sundays may mean being at church all morning—for choir practice, Sunday school, and worship. Work, concerts, and whatever didn't get done during the week take up the afternoon and evening. Many people have little sense of "sabbath" left.

Someone has said, "What lies behind us and what lies before us are tiny matters compared to what lies within us."[1] Being re-created requires time and intentionality. When God blessed and hallowed the seventh day, it was surely not because God couldn't think of anything else that needed doing! Sabbath rest lies at the core of what it means to be created human beings intended to live in harmony with God and all creation. When we are too busy with our agendas to focus on Whose we are, we become less than God created us to be.

Farmers know that soil needs time to rest, so they practice crop rotation and build in fallow time for their fields. Seeds need time to rest in the cool soil before they burst forth to bloom or bear fruit. As we write, we are on sabbatical—a time away from teaching, committee meetings, and advising students—to read and write and think so that we can continue to be productive scholars and teachers. And if the truth be told, everyone needs sabbatical time.

We humans were created to work and play, to work and rest, to work and pray. We were created for relationship—to care for ourselves and others. Hospitality and generosity are kin-dom values. Observing times for worship and re-creative restoration are also kin-dom values. We ignore them at great risk to our physical and spiritual health.

## *Taking Time to Be*

Our lives seem to revolve around doing. All we have to do seems to outstrip our available time and energy. Even our "vacations" can become highly scheduled times of places to go and sights to see. Sometimes we find ourselves returning to work in order to rest from vacation! Even in retirement, friends tell us, "We're busier than ever." We pride ourselves on what we accomplish, on how much we can do. Congregations judge themselves by how many programs they offer, how "active" they are. And our culture, our churches, and our families reward us for this busyness.

Above all, sabbath renewal is taking time to *be*. We do not advocate laziness or avoidance of tasks and ministries that call us to responsible action. Instead, we speak of a balanced life and setting aside times to nourish our being. Both being and doing are important to our discipleship. Within the spiritual life, you can't have one without the other. Our attention to being calls us to doing; our doing grows out of the sense of being we have as individuals and communities of faith. How, then, can we find time to be?

1. *Value sabbath time.* Our achievement-oriented culture places little value on doing nothing. When we can't see evidence that we have accomplished something, we say we have wasted time. The first step to valuing sabbath time comes in recognizing that sabbath is not only the absence of some usual patterns of activity but the presence of time when we can open ourselves to God's renewing presence in our lives. Sabbath concerns itself with "doing something," but that doing does not center in external accomplishments. Rather, sabbath involves attending to our inner

being. Instead of discounting sabbath times as inferior, we must learn to value them.

We and a group of students were at a culture-bridging class in the Santa Fe area; we were visiting the home of a pueblo couple. Our students were full of questions. The hostess finally said, "We need to be quiet for a while so I can get to know you."

Most of us are so busy talking and doing that no space remains for being aware of ourselves, let alone being aware of the presence of others and God. Do we want to get in touch with the interconnectedness of our deepest selves, our community, our world, and our God? Busyness as usual won't do that for us. We must decide if we are happy with the way things are, or if we yearn for a deeper reality enough to value it over the sheer busyness of life.

Sometimes a moment of mystery, a revealing resurrection, an incursion of God's syncopated grace grasps us, and we find ourselves face-to-face with that deeper reality. But suddenly the phone rings, someone's at the door, a deadline must be met, and we let the gift slip through our fingers. Our concern with the urgent leaves no time for the important.

John Hull has published three books about his experience of becoming blind as an adult.[2] Hull's blindness brought about a drastic revision of his priorities. We may choose not to revise ours, but we may miss an important opportunity if we decide to go on as if we can see just fine! Certainly Saul's experience on the road to Damascus called for seeing in a totally new way. (See Acts 9.) He had to let go of his passion for persecuting Christians; they challenged his understanding of his Jewish faith. Christians are often called on to let go of long-held assumptions in order to see what God is calling us to be and to do.

We must first decide whether sabbath time is an important part of the times and seasons of our lives. Sometimes the need for sabbath may grasp us; sometimes we may choose it. But, unless we value it, we may lose its potential significance for our lives. We may be so busy "doing the Lord's work" that we lose the connection with God that keeps us in relationship and on the path of faithfulness.

2. *Identify what nourishes your being.* Not all individuals and communities of faith are alike. We easily forget our uniquenesses as we search for prepackaged programs that have "worked" somewhere else or vigorously advocate that everyone else do what has "worked" for us. Getting up early in the morning to pray will not be spiritually productive for everyone (John Wesley notwithstanding!). We are fed by different options and in different ways.

Our eldest son, Mark, joined our family at age fourteen. He had been in various homes and schools the year before, and one of them had been rigorous about "keeping sabbath" on Sunday. Since he knew we were "preacher folk," he no doubt wondered what the rules would be. He observed that we changed out of our "church clothes" when we got home at noon on Sundays, and we didn't implement the same kind of rigid rules he had known before. After living with us for awhile, Mark concluded that for us, what was appropriate on Sunday depended on the person. He said, "Dad can garden on Sunday because he enjoys that, but it would just be work for me. I can paint the house because I like to paint, but it would be work for Dad."

It's more complicated than that, though, isn't it? Gardening sometimes nourishes and renews. But sometimes, when the weeds get ahead of you, it's just plain work. Yet underneath Mark's comments lies a deep truth. Sabbath time involves nourishing our inner being with God's grace; it connects us with God and all of creation.

That doesn't mean "anything goes." We easily confuse sabbath with "what I like to do." The appropriate understanding of sabbath is closer to "what I *need* to do" to nourish my inner being and to strengthen my relationship with the living God. Dwight knows that working with plants puts him in touch with creation, and through them, with the Creator. He finds looking at their beauty, caring for them, and responding to their growth and their needs restful activities. Clearly at least part of gardening can be a sabbath experience for Dwight. As for whether painting the house is a sabbath sacrament, Mark will have to assess that!

Sometimes persons may need to escape to the golf course or to go for a quiet walk alone in the woods. Sometimes a night out with friends is just what we need. But sabbath time differs from escaping life's pressures. Finding sabbath involves creating space so that God's grace can find a receptive home in us. It may involve real struggle and challenge. We believe that sabbath time requires us to lay aside our agendas and to open our hearts and minds to the one who offers hope where there is no hope and a peace that passes understanding.

Sabbath serves as a retreat from the mundane patterns of life, although it may be found in those patterns. We have a friend who finds significant prayer and meditation time while doing the dishes because the window over the sink looks out upon the beauty of the forest. Doing the dishes provides "parentheses" for her to do her soul work. Brother Lawrence said much the same thing in his classic conversations with God.[3]

Communities of faith also need to discover what nourishes them. Do they find meaning in times of corporate silence or in listening to individuals pray aloud? Perhaps they find nourishment from reading a scripture passage together and then meditating on it. Or maybe they benefit from spending time on retreats where they practice spiritual disciplines individually and corporately and participate in recreational activities.

Sometimes congregational life seems so programmed that there is no place for sabbath in our life together. How can we intentionally take time apart from the business of running the church and seeing that our choirs, classes, and worship services are functioning smoothly to attend to what God asks of us? We know of one congregation that "fasts" from meetings during Lent while encouraging everyone to use that time for practicing a spiritual discipline.

3. *Intentionally "keep sabbath" by establishing patterns of sabbath time in the day, week, and year.* Even if we learn to value sabbath time, it will happen only infrequently if we don't intentionally set apart such time.

Sometimes this attention to soul nourishing becomes only another entry in our datebooks. Dwight's desert days fed his soul while he was in the parish. But he had to guard against the temptation to focus on reading in preparation for next month's sermons. When we take sabbath time, we need to quiet ourselves and meditate on scripture with no personal agenda other than openness to the Word. In a culture where talking is the name of the game, we need to "be still." Sometimes journaling can help us; at other times it provides just one more place where our words get in the way of what God might wish for us to see and hear.

An open posture may help some persons pay closer attention to the Spirit's work in them. One of our friends has created a special place in her bedroom where she can kneel with arms raised or hands palm up and open. She begins and ends each day by spending quiet time with God.

Candles, incense, flowers or a growing plant, a special icon, a cross, a Bible, or some other visual symbol may help us open ourselves to God's Spirit. A wall in our bedroom displays icons and a crucifix from Spain; in front of it sits a glass-topped table with candles. This setting grounds our being as we pray morning and evening prayers, and as we enter or leave our bedroom.[4] Often these prayer symbols are the last items Linda sees at night and the first ones she sees in the morning, providing quieting "bookends" for each day.

Some of our former students save their Christmas cards and letters. Throughout the year, they pull out a card or letter at the breakfast table and talk about what that person or family means to them. Then they pray for this person or family, writing a brief note to share their thanks for how God gifts them through this relationship. We see this practice as a sabbath discipline for this family. They focus on the gifts they receive through relationships across the years.

As we have already seen, Jesus understood the need for time apart to pray and to discern God's will. He spent forty days in the wilderness after his baptism by John. He sought to take his disciples to a place apart after they learned of the beheading of John the Baptist. He took Peter, James, and John up the Mount of Transfiguration, where they encountered God. He went to the garden of Gethsemane to pray just before his arrest.

Certainly we need regular times away where we can step back from the relentless demands that do not allow us time to reflect, think, and pray. We need to reassess, to listen for voices that perhaps are being drowned out by the powerful and articulate, to dare to look at our priorities and assumptions through Christ's eyes. We are not called to keep the letter of the law! Jesus made that abundantly clear. But we are called to acknowledge our humanity and to recognize that even God set aside one day out of seven for rest. How can we do less?

Keeping sabbath, while not easy, is necessary. Everyone needs daily, weekly, and yearly sabbath times. We try to share the daily office each morning and evening. We pray before meals. We hunger for the Eucharist, which is more readily available weekly during the school year when we are teaching at the seminary than at other times. We seek a worshiping community where we can participate in Sunday morning worship. Once a month we attend a covenant group meeting where we share a meal, talk about what is happening in our lives, and pray together. When we travel or find ourselves unable to worship, our rhythm gets off-kilter.

We find larger blocks of re-creative time in the summer

months when we try to intentionally take time to be. Yet we know that we can't store up "being" during the summer and expect it to see us through the hectic school year.

Each individual needs to evaluate his or her own commitment to sabbath and to create space for God to be able to get a word in. What works for one person may not work for another. While there is no one right way to observe sabbath, we rightly seek ways to set apart minutes, hours, and days so that God's grace might enter our consciousness, empowering us to be and do what God calls us toward.

4. *Open yourself to syncopated times of sabbath grace, God's surprises.* While intentionally setting aside sabbath time is important, some sabbath times come as surprises. We hadn't planned for them and often don't want them, but they come anyway!

Perhaps an illness, accident, or another change in our life suddenly leaves us with an enforced "time out!"—not because we have behaved badly but because that's what the game of life involves right now. Will this pause be just a time for doing nothing, or will having nothing to do give us the opportunity for sabbath? Will we see it as an opportunity to reexamine our priorities and evaluate how we spend our lives?

Some of these times of syncopated grace may be relatively brief, and frequently we may respond to them with frustration, annoyance, or impatience. Our phone call is put on hold; we get caught in a traffic jam; we have to wait for a long freight train to clear the crossing. These situations don't seem to offer much potential for grace, but sometimes God surprises us. Suddenly we have time to pray.

We see an item in God's creation that we always hurried past before. Allowing God to surprise us in some of the frustrating times of life can become a treasured gift.

Sometimes unexpected sabbath times provide an oasis of peace. During a particularly busy school term, we took time out to visit good friends. That in itself would have been sabbath time. But we got snowed in, and that time while visiting the home of hospitable friends with nothing that had to be done, was treasured sabbath time. With Jim and Mary, we talked, looked out the window at the falling snow, drank tea, read, and soaked in the gentle quietness in which God's presence could restore our souls. It was a time of deep peace.

## Seasons of Shalom

We often think of peace as the absence of conflict. However, the Hebrew word *shalom* (translated as "peace" in our Bibles) has a much more comprehensive meaning. Basically it means "wholeness" and includes relationships of daily life as well as of society as a whole. It implies "the spiritual completeness of the covenant."[5] *Shalom* includes removal of estrangement from others, ourselves, and God. It describes restored relationship; thus it implies justice. *Shalom* is God's blessing through the gift of wholeness.

*Shalom* is the word the New Testament uses as a greeting both when meeting and when parting. Jesus greeted the disciples and sent them forth with this word. (See Mark 5:34; Luke 7:50; John 20:19-21.) *Shalom* communicates much more than hello or good-bye; it also invokes God's blessing of wholeness.

Sabbath times are seasons of *shalom*. We do not mean that seasons of *shalom* are times during which conflict is absent or occasions of spiritual quietude during which nothing happens. Sabbath times are rich and full, pregnant with meaning. At such times we experience abundant life as individuals and communities, life the way God means it to be. Far from being an escape from "real life," sabbath as *shalom* immerses us in the interconnectedness of a creation made whole by God's grace. For a moment, a time, sometimes even a season, we sense what the kin-dom of God is all about.

The service of death and resurrection for eighteen-year-old Jennifer Purdy may seem like an unlikely time of sabbath *shalom*. The hearts of family, friends, congregation, and community were breaking in the face of that unexpected tragedy.[6] Even though Jenny's service was scheduled for 10:30 A.M. on January 14, 1991, many people had arrived by 9:00. We needed to be with others whose hearts were breaking.

We've already told you that Jenny had been in Spain on a Rotary exchange. She had told her family she had missed hearing familiar Christmas carols. So the evergreen garland had been rehung in the chancel, and the chimes in the tower rang out the Christmas melodies that Dubuque, Iowa, had heard for seventy-eight Christmases. In the midst of our grief we heard the organ prelude, "Jesu, Joy of Man's Desiring," and an organ and piano duet based on "Joy to the World." We heard the words:

> We have gathered here to praise God, and to witness to our faith as we celebrate the life of Jennifer Purdy. We come

together in grief, acknowledging our human loss. May God grant us grace, that in pain we may find comfort, in sorrow hope, and in death resurrection.[7]

As water was sprinkled toward the casket, we recalled that "in baptism Jennifer put on Christ" and prayed "so in Christ may Jennifer be clothed with glory." We heard scripture and witness and prayer.

And we sang "Lord of the Dance," the "Gloria Patri," "On Eagle's Wings," and "Pass It On." We sang "through our tears; in spite of our tears; beyond our tears. The pain was unbelievably intense; yet we had to sing! We held one another; we raised our voices to God."[8]

After the dismissal with God's blessing, the organist played Handel's "Hallelujah Chorus" as the casket was carried out the center aisle, and in the silence that followed we heard the tower chimes playing "Amazing Grace." We heard more testimony in music: a tape of "Oh, but on the Third Day" by Wynton Marsalis as the family exited, and Bach's "Sheep May Safely Graze" as the rest of us followed.

What makes this service a memory of sabbath *shalom* for us is not the absence of pain and grief—far from it. Rather, in the very presence of that grief came the assurance of God's amazing grace. "Joy to the world"—wait just a minute, what joy? Isn't that false and inappropriate? Shouldn't it be "grief to the world"? No, for "the Lord has come," and so we dare to say "Hallelujah" because we remember what happened "on the third day." We know that just as in baptism we put on Christ, so in Christ we will be clothed in glory. And this time of sabbath *shalom* affirms the truth that "neither death, nor life, nor angels, nor rulers, nor things present, nor things to come, nor powers, nor height, nor depth, nor anything else in all creation, will be able to separate us from the love of God in Christ Jesus our Lord" (Rom. 8:38-39).

# *Notes*

1. This quotation has been attributed to Ralph Waldo Emerson and Oliver Wendell Holmes and less frequently to Walt Whitman and Henry David Thoreau. The reference librarians we consulted said that the most proper attribution would be "Anonymous."

2. John M. Hull, *Touching the Rock: An Experience of Blindness* (New York: Vintage Books, 1992); *On Sight and Insight: A Journey into the World of Blindness* (Oxford: Oneworld Publications, 1997); and *In the Beginning There Was Darkness: A Blind Person's Conversations with the Bible* (Harrisburg, Pa.: Trinity Press International, 2002).

3. See Brother Lawrence, *The Practice of the Presence of God,* a Christian classic available in many editions. Our copy was published in New York in 1895 by Fleming H. Revell Co.

4. We use the volumes of *The Daily Office: A Book of Hours for Daily Prayer after the Use of the Order of Saint Luke,* 5 vols. (Akron, Ohio: Order of St. Luke Publications, 1997–2001).

5. E. M. Good, "Peace in the OT," *The Interpreter's Dictionary of the Bible,* ed. George Arthur Buttrick (Nashville, Tenn.: Abingdon Press, 1962) 3:704–706.

6. For a more complete account, see Linda J. Vogel, *Rituals for Resurrection: Celebrating Life and Death* (Nashville, Tenn.: Upper Room Books, 1996), chapter 3.

7. All quotations from "A Service of Death and Resurrection" are taken from *The United Methodist Hymnal* (Nashville, Tenn.: The United Methodist Publishing House, 1989), 870 ff.

8. See *Rituals for Resurrection,* 42.

# Pentecost Power

*It is a blessed thing to know that no power on earth, no temp-*
*tation, no human frailty can dissolve what God holds together.*
—Dietrich Bonhoeffer
*Letters and Papers from Prison*

In sabbath seasons, we focus on being. In Pentecost times, our focus shifts to empowered doing. However, Pentecost activity is not the frantic, fragmented busyness with which we are all too familiar. Nor does Pentecost power reflect the qualities we have come to expect of power.

The biblical story of Pentecost helps us understand the difference between the power from the Holy Spirit and earthly power. After a revealing resurrection time, the disciples went to an upstairs room and "were constantly devoting themselves to prayer" (Acts 1:14*a*). When the Jewish festival of Pentecost came, "they were all together in one place" (Acts 2:1). Pentecost was a sabbath time for the disciples, an experience not for isolated individuals but for the community. Here we learn that being is not separated from doing. Spirit-empowered action grows out of paying attention to who and Whose we are. It is not the activity of lone rangers but of the entire community of faith.

The dynamic activity that followed Pentecost grew out of the gift of the Spirit. Thus, the resulting "work" was grounded in God's grace. Further, the activity focused not on the doers but on communication with others and service to them.

Pentecost power changed fearful disciples who had been hiding in a locked room into bold proclaimers of Christ's resurrection in spite of serious threats from powerful people. (See Acts 2–4.) Pentecost empowers believers to confess their faith. Douglas Hall suggests that "confessing the faith . . . means 'saying'—whether with words, or deeds, or sighs too deep for either—the one thing that *needs* to be said, then and there."[1]

Control or manipulation of others does not evidence this power. Indeed, Spirit power is manifested in

- the gift of sustaining strength for service,
- the gift of undergirding courage to confront oppression,
- the gift of persistent patience for standing with the grieving and oppressed, and
- the capacity and grace for mutual ministry.

From the time of those first disciples until today, Christians have sought to claim and live out of the Spirit power of Pentecost. As James Baldwin says, "To be with God is really to be involved with some enormous, overwhelming desire, and joy, and power which you cannot control, which controls you. . . . I conceive of God, in fact, as a means of liberation and not a means to control others."[2]

Too often the church has used power to control others.

An emphasis on hierarchical power in churches is all too common, whatever the denomination. Many Christians are working toward more mutual understandings of what it means to be the church of Jesus Christ. Yet we still see denominational leaders who use their power to control the lives of pastors, senior pastors who exercise their power over staff, and pastors who exert power over laity. Nor are laity exempt from power struggles. Whether it is the chair of the administrative board, the entire board of trustees, or the patriarch or matriarch of the congregation who holds no formal office but insists on approving every decision, the use of power to retain control is very much present in congregations and denominations.

This problem is not new. In the early church, not long after Pentecost, the believers prayed for boldness and shared their possessions for the common good. (See Acts 4:23-37.) Paul admonished the church at Corinth about abuses of the Lord's Supper. Rich people had been arriving early to eat and drink while the poor, who had to work and arrived later, went hungry. The rich were using their power and privilege over the poor. (See 1 Corinthians 11:17-22.)

The saying "Power corrupts, and absolute power corrupts absolutely" contains some truth politically, economically, and religiously. The church and individual Christians must continually be called back to the model of servant ministry that Jesus embodied.

As Matthew 19:30 reminds us, "Many who are first will be last, and the last will be first." In the words of Mary's song, God "has brought down the powerful from their thrones, and lifted up the lowly" (Luke 1:52). The Son of

God washes the disciples' feet. Christ is sent to eat with sinners and to lift up the lowly—to save the lost and outcasts of society. One of Jesus' kingdom parables proclaims that the workers hired at five o'clock in the afternoon receive the same pay as those who began working early in the morning. (See Matthew 20:1-16.) Jesus challenged the most religious folks of his day (and ours!) to be less concerned with following the letter of the law and more concerned with doing justice, loving kindness, and walking humbly with our God.[3]

Humility is a key to embodying faith. In our time (and probably in every time, if we could only see clearly) issues that go to the core of what it means to be human and to be Christian divide Christians. In their attempts to be faithful, sincere Christians hold diametrically opposed views about what they perceive as God's will regarding life-and-death issues like homosexuality, abortion, and capital punishment. And Christians have always had such differences of opinion. In the nineteenth century, the issue of slavery so divided Methodists that the church split. More than a century passed before The United Methodist Church was able to hold a service of repentance and reconciliation (during the 2000 General Conference) over its own participation in the sin of slavery.

Peter and Paul did not always agree about eating with Gentiles. Yet each person found a way to do ministry without devaluing the other.

John Wesley reluctantly decided that for the greater good of providing preachers and the Eucharist to people moving to North America, he must go against the teachings and practices of the Anglican Church, in which he was a priest in good standing. He ordained persons for this task, even though he was not a bishop and therefore had no authority to do so. He acted because he believed the needs of God's children in America took precedence over the accepted practice of his church.

Jesus reinterpreted scripture in ways that upset many religious people of his day. When the Pharisees criticized Jesus for not following the cleanliness code found in Jewish law by not washing before dinner, Jesus responded in this way:

> Now you Pharisees clean the outside of the cup and of the dish, but inside you are full of greed and wickedness. You fools! Did not the one who made the outside make the inside also? So give for alms those things that are within; and see, everything will be clean for you.
>
> But woe to you Pharisees! For you tithe mint and rue and herbs of all kinds, and neglect justice and the love of God; it is these you ought to have practiced, without neglecting the others. Woe to you Pharisees! For you love to have the seat of honor in the synagogues and to be greeted with respect in the marketplaces. Woe to you! For you are like unmarked graves, and people walk over them without realizing it. (Luke 11:39-44)

Christians are called to seek faithfully to discern God's will. God's love is broad, generous, and inclusive. We believe that Christians are called to share that love with everyone and to encourage all people to live their lives justly and with humility. As disciples of Christ, we speak out and work for that end with passion and joy! But we need to speak truthfully, openly, and compassionately as we enter into discernment with others in our denomination. We must leave room for persons who believe differently than we do to be in ministry. Likewise, they must leave room for us to live as faithfully as we know how. All of us are called to work to clarify our church's stance on issues in ways that do not coerce or require others to go against their own deep beliefs.

During the Vietnam War, a popular bumper sticker said, "America, Love It or Leave It." That mentality—that if one disagrees strongly with one's nation (or one's denomination), one should leave—goes against what Jesus taught. If no room is left for change, then there is no room for prophets. Early Jewish followers of the Way would have been unable able to proclaim the gospel to Gentiles and to receive them as sisters and brothers without their first being circumcised and becoming Jewish converts. Slaves and their descendants would never have become brothers and sisters in our congregations. Prophetic acts, from the Hebrew midwives who saved Moses to Jeremiah to Jesus to Mary Magdalene to John Wesley to Sojourner Truth to Martin Luther King Jr., would not have been tolerated, and the body of Christ would not be what it is today.

As Christians our tasks are to witness to the gospel as we understand it, listen respectfully to others with different views, go to the Table and pray together, and always remain open to God's Spirit. If we follow Jesus, we do not seek to oust persons who differ from us or wield power over those who have no power in the church.

Jesus did not coerce. Rather, he embodied servant ministry and let his life speak for nonviolence, compassion, inclusion, and obedience as he discerned it. Jesus refused to vie for power or to exercise power over others. Rather, he spent his life healing and teaching, giving and receiving, reframing questions and helping people come to see in new ways. He challenged the powerful and offered a healing touch to lepers, women, and children. He prayed for God to "take this cup from me," then he willingly followed what he discerned God wanted him to do as he assented to his arrest and crucifixion. If we believe that God's Spirit empowered Jesus' life, death, and ministry, we must learn to let the spirit of Christ transfigure our understanding of power and action.

## Claiming Our Gifts

The first disciples knew that their Resurrection/Pentecost experience had changed them. They became empowered to do what they could not do before. They received new gifts, new capacities for going about their ministry and mission. They knew that they had not manufactured these abilities for themselves. The abilities came as grace; thus they were called "gifts."

Gifts are present in our everyday lives. Each individual has the capacity to do some things better than others. We are not equally gifted in music, sports, business, or gardening. Some talents and skills come more naturally to us than others and vice versa. We cannot earn the right to them. If we don't have a "gift," no amount of hard work will guarantee excellence. Yet without claiming the gift and developing it, even the most gifted persons will not maximize their gifts.

As teachers we learned that some students have great

gifts for learning but are lazy and apathetic about those gifts, doing just enough to get by. Articulate students who know how to use language well can learn how to sound as though they have done work they haven't done. On closer examination, their work lacks substance and won't stand up to rigorous scrutiny. Other students may be willing to work hard but can do only barely adequate work.

In teaching piano, Dwight found that music seemed to flow from the fingers of some students. Others could master playing the piano mechanically through hard work, but they never attained a musical sound. In some instances, a period of little progress might be followed overnight by a gift liberated by mastering some hitherto elusive technique.

This is one of the times we'd really like to "play God," for we would dearly love to match a person's gifts with his or her willingness to work at claiming and developing them! But that isn't the way gifts work. Gifts come as grace, unmerited and undeserved. What we do with them is up to us. Those who have a gift and willingly claim it, work to develop it, and use it wisely bring much joy to those of us who teach.

But first impressions about gifts can be misleading. Gifts don't have to be flamboyant to be significant. A student who seems unwilling to contribute to class discussion may have the ability to listen and reflect and may make a quiet, simple observation that is wise and perceptive. Another student who has difficulty with intellectual concepts may have gifts of empathy that will enable him or her to become a beloved pastor. We often tell students as we hand back papers, "This grade does not necessarily reflect your ability to do ministry; it indicates the quality of your work in writing this paper!"

Knowledge of the Bible, theology, worship, and Christian education is important for effective ministry, or we wouldn't be teaching. But the ability to do good academic work does not guarantee that someone can minister well, and that keeps us humble. Helping students—indeed, every member of the body of Christ—discern their gifts for ministry encompasses many areas: the ability to study and understand, empathy, listening, the ability to relate to all sorts of people, spiritual depth and maturity, the ability to integrate the Bible and life, teaching, preaching, administering, and much more.

In writing to the church at Corinth, Paul made some wise observations about the gifts of the Spirit. (See 1 Corinthians 12–14.) He believed that God gives every disciple some gifts. Our challenge is to identify those gifts and to empower each person to contribute his or her gifts for the good of the whole community.

No one receives all the gifts, not even the most gifted among us. We need one another. Paul made it clear that God gives gifts for the sake of building up the community, not to make individuals feel more fulfilled or more highly valued. Indeed, as Paul asserted, "the members of the body that seem to be weaker are indispensable" (1 Cor. 12:22).

Pentecost seasons always relate us to the community of faith, its life, and its mission. Coming to minister in a new setting has always been a Pentecost time for us. Receiving a new pastor is a Pentecost time for congregations as well.

No congregation and no pastor is quite like any other.

Each has his or her own particular gifts. No pastor or congregation has all the gifts. Discerning those gifts, claiming them, and developing those strengths are keys to allowing the Spirit to empower the congregation's life and ministry as pastor, staff, and people work together. Further (and this is something persons who tend to judge churches solely on the basis of numerical growth forget), less obvious gifts and growth are no less important to God's kin-dom.

This does not mean that a congregation can say, "Well, we just don't have a gift for worship (or education or stewardship or hospitality or evangelism or outreach or social justice ministry)." To be the church, a congregation must attend to all these areas. The gifts of a congregation relate to *how* it goes about these expressions of its life. What is this congregation in this particular place at this time in history called to do? What gifts does it bring to accomplish that mission? Whenever a congregation is grasped by the Spirit and lives into its vision of what it is called to both be and do, and when it claims the gifts it has been given for actualizing that vision, it is living in Pentecost time.

What is true of congregations is also true for the individuals within them. While Linda was completing her doctoral work, Dwight was appointed to serve a church in a small (population: 300) Iowa town. The tavern burned to the ground the night after we moved into the parsonage, and that left the Coffee Cup Café, a gas station, a grain elevator, a boarded-up elementary school, and one other small Protestant church. We found an amazing variety and depth in the gifts of folks in that small congregation in that tiny Iowa town.

Every Sunday morning while Dwight prepared for the service, a widow with a gift for growing things came in to arrange flowers for the service. This quiet, unassuming woman wasn't one of those persons who thought she knew how the preacher should do everything! Slowly Dwight learned that asking a few questions would elicit a wealth of wisdom from her. While she was never judgmental, she had amazing insight about the people and dynamics of that congregation. Few people seemed to recognize her gift of insight, but it was important to Dwight as a new pastor.

When the nominating committee met, no one seemed to have any ideas about who might be a good lay leader. Dwight asked, "If something happened to me, to whom would the folks in this congregation turn for support, direction, and leadership?" The words were hardly out of his mouth when most of the committee responded, "Wanita"—the first name of an older woman in the congregation. She held no office in the church, but church members knew Wanita had the spiritual strength that they could count on. They discerned her gifts with an insight that stood the test of time. Though surprised to be asked, Wanita served faithfully and well.

When we made hospital visits while at St. Luke's, patients often told us that Ken—a devoted, retired member of the congregation—had come to see them. When Ken died, the congregation had to decide how to fill the absence of his gifts of listening, care, and presence to hospitalized persons. It took not only Jay and Freeman, who were retired and had often visited with Ken, but a whole team of people to fill the void and keep this ministry alive.

As we claim our gifts, the Holy Spirit works in and through us, sustaining our strength for service, undergirding our courage so we can confront oppression, giving us the patience to stand with the grieving and oppressed, and creating in us the capacity and grace for mutual ministry.

## Embodying Our Faith

The Spirit's empowerment enables us to embody our faith. Faith is not restricted to propositions we affirm, as when we confess our faith with the Apostles' Creed. It concerns how we incorporate faith into the way we live our lives.

Embodying faith concerns itself with much more than the present; it also has ramifications for the future church. When Leonardo Boff considered what it means to live an embodied faith in Latin America, he asserted, "Rather than letting our creativity go up in the smoke of the immediately tangible present, we must have the disciplined love of the prophets and commit our love to a future that we may never see. Like the seed falling into the ground, our bodies must prepare the way for the future."[4]

In the Passion story, Jesus takes up his cross after he is condemned to death. Like the seed, he willingly goes to his death in order to prepare the way for our future.

As we read the Gospel stories, we discover that Jesus established and practiced a pattern throughout his ministry. Not only did he live in this self-giving way, but he challenged his followers to do the same. Christ repeatedly calls his disciples to take up their cross and follow him. (See Matthew 16:24; Mark 8:34; and Luke 9:23.)

Taking up the cross is costly and difficult. Embodying the cross of Jesus involves sacrificing our lives, which we value and don't give up lightly. Taking up this cross, however, is a choice we make, a decision. We have other alternatives, but the Spirit leads us to this choice, this action that is not our personal preference. We also take up the cross for the sake of others. Taking up the cross has nothing to do with choosing to see ourselves or to be seen by others as a martyr.

A common understanding of sacrifice is based on a misconception that can be harmful. We tend to think of sacrifice as pain; the more it hurts, the greater the sacrifice, until the greatest sacrifice of all is death itself.

*A sacrifice is what we offer up.* We may offer our lives to God—our gifts, delights, sorrows, and confusions, as well as our faith. If we encounter times when embodying our faith costs, we willingly follow through, come what may. But the important action comes in offering up our lives. Thus Paul writes: "I appeal to you therefore, brothers and sisters, by the mercies of God to present your bodies as a living sacrifice, holy and acceptable to God, which is your spiritual worship" (Rom. 12:1). The incarnation of God in Jesus Christ calls all who seek to follow him and to be his body— the church—to embody faith so that our lives bring hope to a hurting world and light to the nations.

We can find joy in offering up our lives to God through Jesus Christ. Mary's song that we know as the Magnificat is a song of joy and praise: "My soul magnifies the Lord, and my spirit rejoices in God my Savior." (See Luke 1:46-55.) Peter, James, and John were both awed and filled with joy as they saw Jesus transfigured on the mountain. (See Matthew

17:1-8.) Following Jesus' crucifixion, Mary Magdalene must have felt deep joy when she stood before one she thought was a gardener and he called her by name, "Mary!" (See John 20:11-18.) Those two disciples who walked with the stranger on the road to Emmaus reflected on that conversation and said, "Were not our hearts burning within us while he was talking to us on the road, while he was opening the scriptures to us?" (Luke 24:32).

Before Jesus' death and resurrection, he talked with his disciples about what would happen to him. Jesus used an illustration they could understand: "When a woman is in labor, she has pain, because her hour has come. But when her child is born, she no longer remembers the anguish because of the joy of having brought a human being into the world." Then he said, "So you have pain now; but I will see you again, and your hearts will rejoice, and no one will take your joy from you" (John 16:21-22).

So often, Christians past and present have focused on the pain of sacrifice and have lost sight of the deep and lasting joy of sacrifice. As Isak Dinesen writes in *Babette's Feast:* "We have all of us been told that grace is to be found in the universe. But in our human foolishness and short-sightedness we imagine divine grace to be finite. . . . But the moment comes when our eyes are opened, and we see and realize that grace is infinite."[5] Joy is real and lasting. God offers more than enough for all!

When we embody our faith in seasons of Spirit empowerment, we discover that God sustains us for the ministries of service to which God calls us. In the face of oppression and injustice, we receive the gift of courage to stand firm in opposing the violation of God's kin-dom vision. In addition to courage, we receive persistent patience so that we can stand with the grieving and oppressed at times when "being there" is all we know how to do. All this is embodied with others with whom we share mutual ministry in Christ's name. And if we fail to live long enough to see the vision bloom, we can, nevertheless, affirm with the psalmist,

> Weeping may linger for the night,
>     but joy comes with the morning. . . .
> You have turned my mourning into dancing;
>     you have taken off my sackcloth
>     and clothed me with joy. (Psalm 30:5, 11)

In such seasons we can sing with Charles Wesley:

> See how great a flame aspires,
>     kindled by a spark of grace.
> Jesus' love the nations fires,
>     sets the kingdoms on a blaze.
> To bring fire on earth he came,
>     kindled in some hearts it is;
> O that all might catch the flame,
>     all partake the glorious bliss![6]

# Notes

1. Douglas John Hall, *Confessing the Faith: Christian Theology in a North American Context* (Minneapolis, Minn.: Fortress Press, 1996), 11.
2. James Baldwin, *Nobody Knows My Name: More Notes of a Native Son* (New York: Dial Press, 1961), 136.
3. See Micah 6:1-8. In the Gospels Jesus teaches that welcoming children and even becoming like a child are required of those who will be greatest in God's kin-dom (Luke 9:46-48; Matt. 18:1-5; Luke 18:15-17). Jesus embodied the meaning of following God in these ways: avoiding hypocrisy (Luke 12:1-3); weeping over Jerusalem, which "kills the prophets" (Luke 13:31-35); saving the lost (Matt. 18:10-14); caring for lepers (Luke 17:11-19); eating with tax collectors (Luke 19:1-10); being persuaded to change his mind and to heal the Canaanite woman's daughter (Matt. 15:21-28); and asking a Samaritan woman for a drink (John 4:1-42).
4. Leonardo Boff, "Christ's Liberation via Oppression" in *Frontiers of Theology in Latin America,* ed. Rosino Gibellini (Maryknoll, N.Y.: Orbis Books, 1979), 130.
5. Isak Dinesen, quoted in *Alive Now!* (July/August 1998), 109.
6. From "See How Great a Flame Aspires" by Charles Wesley, 1749, in *The United Methodist Hymnal* (Nashville, Tenn.: The United Methodist Publishing House, 1989), No. 541.

# Resonating Rhythms

*Sacred spacemaking breaks the rhythm of the ordinary and*
*punctuates it with moments of God-consciousness.*
—Kenda Creasy Dean and Ron Foster
*The Godbearing Life*

In previous chapters we have considered the sacramental potential in various times and seasons of our lives. God's syncopated grace may intervene anytime; our experiences become holy when we recognize God's gracious presence in them. Another rhythm resonates with these experiences: the cycle of preparation, celebration, and reflection surrounding the occasions that provide markers for our lives. We usually observe these events with certain rituals.

By "marker events," we are speaking of birthdays, anniversaries, holidays, even weekends and vacations. Some large, extended families gather for Sunday dinners. Not all communities, families, or individuals observe the same calendar of yearly rituals, but everyone we know has them. These rituals, while not sacramental in and of themselves, are seen as special already, and we may learn to recognize them as sacramental.

We prepare for these events and engage in patterns of celebration with them. Later, as Aunt Esther would say, we "live in the afterglow." And we expect them to be a part of our lives year after year, or time and time again. Usually we think of preparation as what we have to do to get ready for the "main event." We often describe the time after the event as a letdown, saying we have to return to work to recover.

Preparation and reflection times can potentially be much more than preface and postscript to the main event or experience. They can carry sacramental value in and of themselves. When we learn to attend to these resonating rhythms of preparation/celebration/reflection, they can help us get in touch with the sacredness in all of life.

## *Preparation Times*

We live in Rogers Park—a religiously and culturally diverse neighborhood on the north side of Chicago. Three blocks from us is a park and beach on Lake Michigan. On the first warm weekend of spring (April, if we're lucky), the beachfront is covered with groups of families and friends who bring portable grills, blankets, CD players, and baskets or boxes of food to set up for the day. Music of all kinds— Spanish, Asian, rap, gospel, rock, Jamaican—fills the air. Children of all colors, speaking many different languages, play on the slides and swings and dig in the sand. There are young and old. Joggers, cyclists, and walkers abound on the sidewalk. Spring has come to the city!

We love to walk along the beach and listen to the symphony of voices and sounds. Lots of preparation went into this day at the beach—preparing food, gathering sunscreen and extra clothes for the kids and jackets for when it gets cool, and finding frisbees that haven't been used since last summer. Often people feel as excited about preparing for this outing as they do about spending the day at the beach.

"Getting ready" times are usually exciting for the two of us. Every year, as we get ready to go to our mountain cabin for the summer, we begin laying aside the clothes and books we want to take with us. Throughout the year we fill a suitcase in our storeroom with items we don't want to forget.

Weeks before our winter break at Sanibel Island, we ask our traveling companions Paul and Carol, "Have you started getting ready yet?" And the answer may be, "Oh, no, not yet, it's too early . . . except for that little pile of things on the dresser in the guest room!"

Dwight loves to plan our trips abroad. He reads the guidebooks, pores over maps, and then lays out several choices of activities. He loves to think about the details. He even studies the map to determine whether we should turn left or right when we leave the Dublin airport in our rental car! We hardly ever have a day when we follow the preplanned agenda exactly; we feel free to change it as we go along. That's why we've discovered that the joy of planning the trip is not merely a function of deciding what we will do when and where. It is the excitement of thinking about what we might do, even if we decide later not to do it. Anticipation can bring as much joy as the event or celebration itself.

A year before Linda's sixtieth birthday, Dwight began to plan. What does she love to do? Take train rides! Where does she like to go? Santa Fe is a favorite place. Why not make reservations for a long weekend train ride in a sleeping compartment and spend a couple of days in Santa Fe?

But then what about the friends and family she'd want to have with her when she celebrates? What if the next weekend, they came to Chicago for a surprise celebration? They could be in our home when we get back from the symphony concert Friday night. We could have brunch the next morning, go out for dinner at a restaurant of her choice, and then return home for dessert, where she is surprised yet again with more folks from the Chicago area coming in for an open house. *How much of this can I pull off as a surprise?* Dwight wondered. But then Dwight let Linda ask one question a day, and she guessed about the train ride in advance, which diverted her attention from all the surprises coming the next weekend. In addition, she got much joy from anticipating the train trip and seeing our friends in Santa Fe.

Looking back on it, Dwight experienced real joy in planning, in getting ready, in dreaming about what could happen, and then in laying the groundwork for making it happen. Joyous anticipation is delightful!

We can miss that joy if we become overly anxious about what might go wrong. Often what happens isn't as bad as we fear. *What if Linda finds out about the train trip?* She did, and as a result she was able to share in the anticipation. *What if plans for our friends to get into our home while we are at the symphony don't work out?* They did get in, but if they hadn't, we suspect our doorbell would have rung soon after we got home, and that would also have been a surprise.

Too often we allow worry to consume us, or we take on too much responsibility and feel hassled and overwhelmed instead of enjoying these times of preparation. When we can view times of preparation as valuable and as holding the potential for joy, they may become sacramental in their own right. We can see God at work with and through us as we journey through these holy times.

Gardeners know about preparation times too: getting everything ready, planting, watering, weeding, watching for the first green shoots to emerge or the dormant bush to bud. The smell of dirt, the sound of garden tools raking or digging in the soil, and breathing in the fresh air of spring are treasures to be savored.

Hidden behind the obvious activities of preparation, we may discover the sacred: an awareness of God's presence may be revealed to us. When we recognize it as a gift, we can respond with gratitude. The God above and beyond us is present with us in our watching and waiting, our planning and preparing, our anticipation and expectation.

## Festivals of Celebration

Families and groups of friends arrive at the beach and choose their favorite spot. They may put up a tarp or arrange their folding chairs and set up grills. Children sit on the ground and take off their shoes—at last they can go barefoot! They run across the grass and onto the sandy beach. Boom boxes crank up, and some folks grab a soda from the cooler and head for the nearest chair. Others begin tossing a frisbee. There is often banter among the groups of folks who have come to camp out for the day. Spring has come to the city, at least for this day!

The day arrives; the time comes for the celebration. Or we arrive at our destination, rent the car, and head toward our first bed-and-breakfast. Or the flowers burst into bloom, filling the air with their fragrance. What we have been waiting for, anticipating, expecting, has arrived.

The occasion doesn't have to be spectacular. One year, early in our marriage, finances were tight when our wedding anniversary rolled around. We didn't have money for our usual weekend getaway celebration. However, we took advantage of a family member's offer to care for our kids, and we set out to go camping at a nearby state park. Dwight lighted a fire in the drizzle and Linda prepared shish kebabs inside our VW camper. That's all. Ah, but if you think the occasion wasn't special, you're wrong! Never has a meal tasted so good, in spite of the cold and rain. We were happy just being together, delighting in what we shared. We can't tell you the menu for any other anniversary dinner we've shared in forty-three years of married life, but we remember that celebration in detail: the aroma; the taste; the beauty of the hills around us; the damp, cold air; the gift of quiet togetherness. When we told that story, our nurse friend Mary Purdy said, "Of course! One of the basic facts we know about the brain is that we remember best those experiences that are coupled with emotion."

At such times, past, present, and future are dynamically present. Let's look at one of the great celebrations of the Christian community to see how it combines these three dimensions of time. When we celebrate the Eucharist (also called the Lord's Supper or Holy Communion), we remember what Jesus said and did at his Last Supper with his disciples. We may also recall how he fed the five thousand. We recall his crucifixion, but as an Easter people we affirm that "the risen Christ is with us."[1] So we also remember how he ate with those two disciples from Emmaus after the Resurrection and how he shared a fish breakfast on the shore with his disciples just before he ascended into heaven.[2]

Moreover, sharing the bread and cup is not just an action to trigger our memory, but it offers us something vital and significant *now*. "The bread which we break is a sharing in the body of Christ." We are the body of Christ. We expect something to happen to us here and now, so we pray: "Pour out your Holy Spirit on us gathered here, and on these gifts of bread and wine. Make them be for us the body and blood of Christ, that we may be for the world the body of Christ, redeemed by his blood."

The future is also present in this celebration because the Eucharist concerns what we will be doing and where we are going. So we pray: "By your Spirit make us one with Christ, one with each other, and one in ministry to all the world, until Christ comes in final victory and we feast at his heavenly banquet." Our celebration interweaves past, present, and future.

Celebrating Eucharist also connects us with memories and hopes for ourselves, our families, and our congregations. We remember sharing in Eucharist as our first act as husband and wife at our wedding; we remember receiving Communion at funerals and on Holy Thursday and Christmas Eve. Whenever we celebrate Eucharist, we bring to the Table with us the joys and sorrows in our lives, as well as those from the life of the church and world through the ages.

A few years ago we celebrated our fortieth anniversary as life partners. We renewed our wedding vows with our covenant prayer group. Rather than holding one big celebration, we invited friends and family to spend time with us at our cabin throughout the summer so that we could really enjoy their presence. What goes on in an anniversary celebration like that?

Some of the celebration relates to the past. We remember our wedding—laughing at our hairstyles and bemoaning how much more of us there is to love now than then! At our renewal of vows, Dwight sang the same prayer he had sung at our wedding. However, this is an anniversary of our life vows to each other in the sight of God and our family and friends. So the wedding itself is not central; rather, the marriage. The focus is not just one event in the past but all the joys and tears, the burdens and delights, the hurts and comforts we have shared. The past serves as more than prologue; it is part of who we are here and now. An anniversary offers a couple the opportunity not only to give gratitude for the past but also to recommit in the present. To repeat our vows to each other before God affirms that they are not just a relic of bygone times but rather the pattern out of which and into which we live. Nor does the relationship stop with this present moment. We move into the future with our relationship, still growing and developing. Love doesn't stand still; it either deepens or it withers.

Love, we have come to understand, is always a gift, always grace. We do not earn or deserve love, but love calls for a gift of love in return. We can squander love or nourish it. Sometimes it is unutterably delightful; sometimes it is painful beyond words. At times it requires hard work. But often loving each other is the easiest and most natural thing we do. The rich, complex fabric of married life is sacramental for us. Marriage encompasses memories, the present moment, and hope for the future. Anniversaries lift us once again out of the busyness of our daily lives so that we can remember, give thanks, recommit, and hope as we thank God for one another and our shared life. When we celebrate anniversaries in this way, we engage in sacramental living.

We come to recognize the sacredness of our covenant love. God is present in our relationship with each other, both transcendent (beyond) and immanent (within) our life partnership. We express profound gratitude for this gift, but this sacrament of love also demands a response: nothing less than the commitment of all we are.

Instead of treasuring the passing moment of celebration, it is possible to pass by the moment in our concern for other things. We're always perplexed by folks who seem to miss out on the wedding, the vacation, or the family dinner because they are so intent on capturing the moment on film. Often people miss participating in the event for the sake of preserving future "memories."

Linda's entire family deeply loves Marvin, her stepfather. He was born on December 25, and his birthday always seemed to get overshadowed by Christmas. Somehow we learned that he had never in his life had a birthday party, and Linda and her sisters decided to change that. Exactly one month before his eighty-fifth birthday, Linda's entire family traveled to Kansas City. Linda's folks were expecting most of us for Thanksgiving dinner, so our (Dwight and Linda's) presence wasn't a surprise when we arrived the evening before. We always stayed in a basement overflow room (our folks' quarter of the basement under their four-plex). As the other adult children and their children slipped in under the cover of darkness early on the morning of November 25, Linda's folks were unaware. We decorated the downstairs with balloons and streamers and set up a table with coffee, juice, and coffee cake.

We (Dwight and Linda) went upstairs shortly before breakfast and said to Mother and Dad, "Come quick and be quiet! We have something to show you!" They had seen a fox with her babies from a window well once before, so they came downstairs to see if that is what we had seen. The surprise gathering overwhelmed them both. It was a time of gratitude for Marvin's life, a celebration of his love, an affirmation of a future rich in relationship. A month later Dad wrote a letter of thanks to his "second" family, saying, "Now I'm shooting for ninety so you can surprise me again!"

## Seasons of Reflection

For some, when the day at the beach is over, that is that. But many reflect and reminisce: "The air was so crisp and clear today!" "We could see the whole city skyline and the Sears Tower from the fishing pier!" "I loved hearing the waves lap against the pier!" "Wasn't the lake beautiful?" "Didn't it feel great to watch that family building that sand castle?" "The kids really seemed to enjoy playing on the slides and swings—and they laughed and managed to communicate even when they all couldn't speak Spanish!"

Some saw God's grace in the experience. Some only recognized that it was a great day. But recognized or not, celebrations like this hold the potential for being syncopated with grace.

What happens after the celebration, after we return from the trip, after the party is over? After Dad's birthday party, some of the party decorations came down, but when we returned later that winter some balloons were still bouncing, while others sagged a little from the ceiling rafters where we had tacked them. In fact, the following May when we went home for his funeral celebration, some of the balloons were still there, reminding us of his first-ever birthday party!

Right after a celebration, many things need to be done: cleaning up, putting away, letting life get back to "normal." Yet those "balloons" on the ceiling—reminders of the celebration event—remain. Linda makes albums of photos taken on our trips, and we relive those experiences over and over again. "Relive"—that's more than remembering, isn't it? It's a way to recognize the impact of the past on our present.

The early church devoted the time after the yearly celebration of the Resurrection (Easter) to *mystagogy*. Mystagogy is the process of coming to understand the meaning of the mysteries of baptism and Eucharist, those great symbols of death and resurrection, for each individual and for the church—Christ's body. It is a time for pondering the question, "What difference does all this make?"

During reflection times we may first realize that our preparation and celebration times have been sacramental. As we think about them, we say: "It was a holy time"; "God was there"; "That was a real gift"; "What a difference that's made!" In times of reflection and appropriation, we come to a conscious recognition of just how life-transforming and life-nourishing these events have been and can be. Naming and claiming the holy in our everyday lives and in our times of preparation and celebration helps us recognize the holy when we see it again in different times and places. Once we recognize God's mystery in the mist lying in the valley and name it, we are more likely to see God in our next experience of morning mist. Seeing the sacramental is itself a sacramental gift.

## Facing Death Leads to Life

Marvin had written that he was shooting for age ninety so we could give him another party. But several years earlier when he had come close to dying, Marvin had told Linda's mother that he planned to enjoy every minute he had left, but whenever the time came for him to die, he was ready. We spent Mother's Day weekend with Mother and Dad and had a wonderful time. A week later, we got one of those dreaded phone calls—we learned that an aneurysm had burst in Marvin's brain, and he had been rushed to the hospital. Now our family faced a decision: whether to let a respirator sustain Marvin's breathing or to remove him from life support. Marvin had been clear that when his time came, he was ready to meet his Maker. Painful though it was, we agreed to have him removed from life support.

So that wonderful birthday party became our family's send-off for Dad—he knew how much we loved and cared for him in no uncertain terms. And his thank-you letter to us put into words what his life embodied—that he was our dad who loved us as his own, and we were his family too.

Dad's service of death and resurrection celebrated the loving, giving person he was. We grieve our loss even as we celebrate his wholeness. How grateful we are that he was active and well until the moment he died.

Reflecting on our baptism and seeing it as dying and being made new can prepare us for our physical deaths. Death loses its power over us, and we know the truth of what Paul said—"if we live, we live to the Lord, and if we die, we die to the Lord, so then, whether we live or whether we die, we are the Lord's" (Rom. 14:8).

## Life Reconstruction

Preparation, celebration, and reflection are all syncopated with moments of grace for those who are open to the Spirit's gifts. Learning to recognize these grace-filled moments is part of what it means to engage in sacramental living.

At times we feel that our world has come to an end: a marriage ends; a child or a parent dies; a single mom loses her job because of alcoholism; a son, daughter, or spouse is arrested. The list goes on and on. When something drastic occurs, we cannot continue as if nothing has happened. Drastic changes require reconstruction—we must put our lives together in new ways.

For a time, some persons may live in denial, acting as if nothing has happened and refusing to face the loss and the changes it requires. Others may abdicate responsibility for dealing with the changes and become apathetic and/or dependent on another. But for most people—folks who desire to put their lives back together as best they can—life reconstruction is called for.

Marvin died. Linda's mother—now widowed for the second time—had to engage in life reconstruction. And even in that process, there were many holy moments—sorrow was syncopated with grace-filled gifts. The baby robins Mother and Dad had watched from the time the eggs were laid flew from the nest the day of Dad's funeral! Friends told us stories about Dad that made us smile or laugh or cry—stories that characterized his gracious and warm way of being with folks. Mother found a poem among his papers, addressed to her and her daughters and their families, that expressed his deep love for us all. Finding that poem weeks after his death touched our grief with grace-filled syncopation. Mother called and read it over the phone to us, and we all cried—tears of sadness and joy.

It is hard to imagine grieving without moments of syncopated grace that break in on our sense of loss and sadness. Persons who suffer senseless violence, such as the shooting deaths of innocent children, find themselves living in a world gone awry. Spouses who learn of the violation and deception of a spouse who recklessly disregards wedding vows and commitments to children in the family must deal with life-wrenching anger as well as loss and sadness. Sometimes persons who break vows experience judgment and anger from folks who only know one side of the story and who ignore the deep pain that led them to such actions.

For the third time across the years, we spent Good Friday visiting the Santuario de Chimayó, a small Spanish chapel built on a site that has been known for hundreds of years as a healing place. It is a place we are drawn to as well. We experience it as one of those "thin places"³ where one senses deeply the presence of God.

Pilgrims walk from as far away as Albuquerque and Santa Fe; many of them walk through the night on Thursday in order to arrive at the little church on Good Friday. As we watched the pilgrims on their journeys and walked among them around Chimayó, it was a solemn, joyous time.

Families make the journey together for many different reasons. We saw babies on parents' backs, in wagons, and strollers. Teenagers sing as they walk along together. We observed one strong teenage boy with his arm around an older woman who could have been his grandmother, helping her as they trudged along.

No doubt, for many this pilgrimage is a spiritual discipline—a time to reflect and pray. Some walk to give thanks to God for healing in their lives; others make the trek on crutches or in wheelchairs as they pray for healing. Some carry heavy crosses.

One fifty-three-year-old Vietnam veteran who has made this annual pilgrimage for over twenty years shared his story with a feature writer for the *Albuquerque Journal*.⁴ The veteran's journey begins at 4:00 A.M. on Good Friday, when he walks to a church in Santa Cruz and attends a prayer service before dawn. As he walks, he pounds the earth with a large wooden staff. Seriously wounded in Vietnam, the veteran says he has twelve holes in his body and suffers from post-traumatic stress disorder. He sees his walking staff "as a therapeutic tool that supports him on his lifelong journey to better mental health." He observes that he continues to learn to deal with his situation "one step at a time." As he walks, he prays for all veterans who died—but especially for his comrades who died in Vietnam. As he said, "You have to observe the day of Christ, meditate on his mysteries and wait for his resurrection on Easter Sunday."

Some folks set up their pickups or card tables along the route from Santa Fe to Chimayó to serve the thousands of pilgrims who pass that way. One stand contains dozens of boxes of free oranges for the walkers. Over the next mile, orange peels dot the side of the road in the high desert landscape, a thanks offering from grateful walkers. Other people hand water to the walkers. Occasionally someone puts up a tarp with folding chairs underneath and beckons travelers to rest in the shade for awhile. Always, these are free gifts for those on the pilgrimage. One roadside encourager told a reporter, "I used to walk like the rest of them, but I got a little heavy on the age and decided to serve them instead."[5]

This experience, shared by folks of all ages, religions, and racial and ethnic backgrounds, powerfully illustrates that preparation, celebration, and reflection cannot be neatly separated. Like the past/present/future, preparation/celebration/reflection interweave in complex ways. The Vietnam veteran still lives with the wounds of his past—and the spiritual and psychological wounds are the deepest of all. His prayers include his comrades who died more than thirty years ago, Jesus' crucifixion and his own journey now with others in his faith community, the coming Resurrection on Easter and his own ongoing healing, and a resurrection future for himself and his family. Preparation time included getting ready physically and spiritually. The walk itself was both a celebration (remembering the Good Friday event) and preparation for Easter. Every time his staff hit the ground, he prayed, reflected, and hoped for healing; for release from pain; for better mental health, which he knows will be a lifelong struggle. This father of eight, devout Roman Catholic, and loyal American lives sacramentally because his journey is syncopated with grace and hope.

## Recognizing Syncopated Grace

According to the Wesleyan understanding of grace, grace is present in each person's life from birth until death without our conscious awareness of it. God's gift touches, nudges, and invites us to take another look—to recognize that the one who creates us wants to be in relationship with us. God's creative act can become a shared act when we open our lives and say yes to the gift of real life with God that is available for every human being.

John Hull, a professor of religious education in England, describes his experience of going blind as an adult like this:

> Blindness is like a huge vacuum cleaner which comes down upon your life, sucking almost everything away. Your past memories, your interests, your perception of time and how you will spend it, place itself, even the world, everything is sucked out. Your consciousness is evacuated, and you are left to reconstruct it. . . . I still think there is something purging about blindness. One must re-create one's life or be destroyed."[6]

John began his faith walk long before he became blind, and faith sustains him through this difficult journey. By sharing his experience with physical blindness, he may help us find a metaphor for humanity's spiritual blindness.

Sometimes it takes a drastic experience (like Saul's on the road to Damascus) for us to see our life as it really is and to set out to recreate our sense of self with God's gracious love at the center of our being. For others, being attuned to God's grace in "the still small voice" enables us to respond and refocus our lives without such a drastic and dramatic conversion experience. But whether one hears God's voice as quiet or booming, in public or private, God invites every person to receive the gift of grace and to respond by sharing the good news of the gospel and living a life of justice and compassion.

Once we recognize God's grace, we reconstruct our lives by dying to self-centeredness and being made new in Christ Jesus. Living as Christ's disciples brings joy, but it also brings challenges and hardships. Our everyday, ordinary journeys continue to be syncopated with grace-filled moments. We see an eagle flying overhead; we receive an e-mail from a friend we had lost touch with; a child smiles shyly at us as we walk down the street; we take time to pray for a friend. Whenever and wherever we become aware of God's presence and care, we are being gifted with grace.

When we focus on how we prepare to celebrate, the celebrations themselves, and the reflections about them afterward, we often discover that the steady beat under and within our lives is enriched by the syncopated grace of God that enlivens the melodies of our living. Sometimes this grace-filled moment is as simple as a butterfly lighting on the casket of a loved one or as awe-inspiring as the night sky transformed with flashes of lightning. But whenever we become aware of God's Spirit breaking in upon us, we are living sacramentally. Our eyes are opened; we recognize that Jesus lives; and because he lives, we too are gifted with life and hope and joy and peace!

## Notes

1. All quotations of language used regarding celebrations of the Lord's Supper come from "A Service of Word and Table I," found in *The United Methodist Hymnal* (Nashville, Tenn.: The United Methodist Publishing House, 1989), 6–11.
2. See Luke 24:13-35 and John 21:1-14.
3. "Thin places" is a Celtic way of speaking of those places where the separation between this world and the world beyond is thin.
4. Daniel J. Chacon, "Wounded Vet on Trek Prays for Comrades Who Served in Vietnam," *Albuquerque Journal*, Saturday, 14 April 2001, 1–2.
5. Deborah Davis, "It's about the Experience," *The Santa Fe New Mexican*, Saturday, 14 April 2001, A-1.
6. John M. Hull, *On Sight and Insight: A Journey into the World of Blindness* (Oxford: Oneworld Publications, 1997), 155.

# Emmaus Epiphanies

*No one knows what lies ahead when we say yes to God! To accept God's invitation to a creative relationship requires learning different rhythms. These rhythms sustain us and pull us into a dance set to the heartbeat of God.*

—Jan L. Richardson
*Sacred Journeys*

Viewing the pattern of our lives in light of the church year helps us understand these times and seasons as sacramental. Each year the church intentionally keeps time with Jesus. The church refers to every Sunday as the Lord's Day. Most Christian congregations celebrate Easter and Christmas, and many also observe Pentecost. Advent and Lent become times of preparation for the great Christian festivals— Christmas and Easter. The church year is not, however, merely a circular journey that ends where it started. It is a pilgrimage. Each Advent we begin the next Christian year from our new place in our faith pilgrimage. We pray that each year finds us more mature and still growing in our faith.

*Pilgrims*, as we use the word, are not just people journeying somewhere. A pilgrimage has distinct characteristics. Pilgrims are *on the way to a holy place*; they do not wander aimlessly. Yet the journey itself is part of that holy endeavor; what happens along the way is not incidental to the pilgrimage. *Both the goal and the pathway toward it are sacred.* Further, one does not undertake a pilgrimage alone but in company with others. A pilgrimage is a *corporate undertaking.*

A pilgrimage involves leaving where you are and moving toward a destination. On a pilgrimage, you have to leave behind some possessions; you can't afford to be bogged down or distracted with excess baggage. You do need to take some items with you. And you expect to find some of what you need along the way.

Every year the church makes pilgrimage. Christians are a people "on the way" to God's kin-dom, where God's way will reign and we will be part of the host who praise God unceasingly. The journey to this holy kin-dom is also sacramental. Together the community of faith walks a way that Jesus Christ made holy in his own pilgrimage. Saints and martyrs have walked this way before us, and the journey both beckons and challenges us to be part of that great company of believers—past, present, and future.

If the pilgrimage is to open for us the way of sacramental living, we must leave behind some assumptions and practices. We are like the American pioneers who left their homes in the east with many treasured possessions, only to have to discard them one by one along the way. They learned that if they didn't lighten their load, they would never reach their destination. Jesus' earliest followers also had to learn this concept. Abstinence from eating meat that was considered unclean seemed central to Peter's faith, but the Holy Spirit helped him discover that he needed to leave behind that core belief and practice so that God's good news could be shared with Gentiles.[1]

Distinguishing between excess baggage and core convictions of our faith is not easy. As we go through life's struggles, we find ourselves brought up short as the Holy Spirit asks us: *Is that really as important as you think? What are the fruits of holding fast to that belief and practice?*

We take with us the faith experience of the past, the heritage that tells the story and helps us remember our way into the future. But much of what we need will be found along the way. That calls for openness to hear God's Word in new ways, willingness to enter into the times and seasons of the church year, being fed at font and Table as we renew our baptismal covenant and share in the eucharistic feast with our brothers and sisters. The journey invites us to offer our experience of God to persons who are different from us and to risk learning from those whose beliefs and practices differ from ours.

This reminds us of the experience of those two disciples walking to Emmaus—a story to which we have referred frequently. They thought they were on a journey. But when Jesus broke bread with them, they recognized that they had really been on a pilgrimage. They let go of their assumptions about the events they had witnessed and dared to walk into a new and holy understanding. Looking back, they realized that they were nourished on the way as their hearts burned within them.

Pilgrimages are sacramental seasons. While the significance of our journey is often not immediately obvious and thus hidden (just as those two disciples did not recognize Jesus on the road), the deeper meaning of our journey comes to be revealed. The deeper meaning of the journey is a gift we receive (our eyes must be opened), yet we must perceive it for ourselves (just as the two disciples from Emmaus recognized Jesus). In sacramental pilgrimages we respond (just as those disciples returned to Jerusalem to bear witness that Jesus had been made known to them in the breaking of bread). Such experiences develop our awareness that the holy is among and within us and yet always beyond us (both immanent and transcendent). They become Emmaus epiphanies for us, breaking open and making manifest the sacramental.

Each of us can recall times when we saw something in a totally new way. We say we had an "aha" experience or we "saw the light." As we let the times and seasons of the church year resonate with our lives, we discover amazing parallels between our personal pilgrimages and the yearly pilgrimage of the church.

Our lives may still be in Lent when the church is celebrating Easter, or we may experience a Christmas moment when the church calendar says it is ordinary time. But when we name our own experiences as individuals and communities of faith in terms of the liturgical year, we create a new context and perspective for viewing our experience, which can deepen our understanding both of what we do in worship and what is happening in our lives.[2]

## Ordinary Time

While we started our journey with the mundane meanderings of ordinary time, the church year teaches us that we understand ordinary time best in light of Jesus' death and resurrection. Laurence Stookey says, "Because of what has been made known in Christ, no time can again be regarded as ordinary in the sense of dull or commonplace. . . . Christ has sanctified all of time, bringing us and the whole of our experience into the orbit of resurrection. What we deem ordinary, God has transformed into the extraordinary by the power of divine grace."[3]

Every Sunday in ordinary time is a feast of resurrection. It embodies the heart of why we worship on the Lord's Day. And every ordinary day of our lives is syncopated with the Christian affirmation, "Christ lives!"

The extraordinary is present in the midst of the everyday. God works not only on the mountaintops or in the valleys but also on the level ground, where the road reaches from horizon to horizon.

In the two great cycles of the church year (Advent/ Christmas/Epiphany and Lent/Easter/Pentecost), Christians participate in the mystery of God's saving work through the central events of our sacred history. Ordinary time challenges us to see God's saving activity in the common, the mundane. We come to recognize that the symbols of our great festivals are grounded in the ordinary: a manger, a cross, a tomb, light, water, bread, and cup.

To fully appreciate divine grace, Claus Westermeyer tells us, we must look at both the great epiphanies of salvation we find in high holy days and seasons and the blessings of God's continuing and abiding presence.[4] In the everyday ordinary we can become aware of God's presence and know that presence to be extraordinary.

When the tasks before us seem greater than our time

and energy, when we lose sight of meaning and purpose and hope, or when depression settles in, we often travel for long periods in ordinary time. Sometimes ordinary time feels like we are on a treadmill—putting one foot in front of the other, doing what needs doing, surviving. At other times, it can be a time of quiet, steady growth. Life seems to be moving in a positive direction at a normal pace. We work, we learn, and we worship as ordinary day follows ordinary day.

Even so, we know that sometimes even the Lord's Days, which punctuate ordinary life with reminders of extraordinary grace, become a part of the flat landscape where just keeping on is itself a victory. Daring to hold on as we keep doing what needs doing sometimes takes greater courage than taking obvious risks with high stakes. The miracle is that even then, God's syncopated grace can intrude into the routine or relentless patterns of the ordinary.

## Advent

Our secular culture seems intent on making Advent into Christmas. Many churches face an uphill battle in the church's countercultural insistence that Advent has value in and of itself. Their members can become quite perturbed at attempting to understand Advent as something other than the elongation of Christmas festivity.

We need to reclaim Advent as a season of preparation for the celebration of the nativity. Such a time of preparation has its own resonance with the rhythms of our lives (see chapter 7). Advent should be more than a period of preparation; it also encompasses a *longing for things to be different*. This deep longing, coupled with *watching* and *waiting*, characterizes Advent times in our lives.

For many in our culture, this longing for things to be different may be foremost in their thinking as they feel overwhelmed with Christmas preparations—decorating, shopping, mailing packages, sending cards or letters, entertaining—and keeping up with the regular activities of life. But they fail to see that this longing could provide the answer they seek. Building more quiet time into Advent is possible. We don't have to do all the tasks we think we must do. We can focus on what it means to walk toward and into God's kin-dom. When we do that and focus on the coming (again) of Jesus into our hearts and our world, Advent becomes a time of quiet joy and hope. We find that we have reprioritized what needs doing as we prepare for Christmas.

Parents awaiting the birth of a child provide one example of such a time of waiting, hoping, and preparing. As adoptive parents, we recall an Advent season in the summer of 1967. Linda often sat on the front porch swing waiting for the mail, eagerly anticipating word about receiving a baby into our family. The nursery was prepared; the name was chosen. We knew that our family of four would soon become a family of five and life would be different.

Many students experience the last months of seminary as an Advent time while they await word of the churches they will serve. Churches also experience this time of waiting, wondering, hoping, and preparing as they await a new pastor, move into a new or remodeled building, or begin a new ministry.

Our world, our nation, and our churches all long for different situations. Whenever we long for peace, justice, an end to oppression, a cessation to the abuse of power, the acceptance of the sacred worth of all God's children, whether in our congregations or our individual lives, we live in an Advent season.

The church's observance of Advent has three affirmations: "Christ came; Christ comes; Christ will come again." Sometimes during Advent we become startled when the Bible readings refer to the Second Coming rather than to the Bethlehem birth. For the church, the scripture readings are all part of the proclamation of God's saving acts in Jesus Christ. In the midst of our deep longing, our watching and waiting, we remember that Christ came to us on that first Christmas, and we prepare to celebrate that coming. But we also anticipate the future time of Christ's coming when God's kin-dom will come and God's will be done on earth as in heaven.

Advent also reminds us that we do not live in a time of the absence of Christ, caught in an arid desert between the times of the First and Second Comings. When our eyes are opened and our hearts burn within us, the presence of Jesus is made known to us in the breaking of bread—through both Word and Table. As we long for that presence, watching and waiting and preparing for it to change our lives, our churches, our communities, and our world, we can know we are living in a sacramental time of Advent.

## Christmas and Epiphany

In chapter 1, we pointed to the potential of Christmas to reclaim its power as more than a secular holiday. Most of us probably decorate for Christmas. But because cards, cookies, decorations, and trees are all special—different from what we usually see and do—we can easily miss what is at the heart of Christmas as a sacramental season in our lives.

Think again about the story in Luke's Gospel: no room at the inn, a birth in a stable, an animal's feed box for a baby bed. Smelly shepherds were the first to be told of Jesus' birth. The persistent theme of Christmas is the presence of the holy in common, ordinary situations and people.

God's trumpeting Word reminds us that, like Herod and the religious people of Jesus' day, we often look in the wrong places and expect the spectacular when God can be found in humble surroundings and people. God's "still small voice" is often drowned out because we listen to the loud, booming, powerful voices. Whenever we recognize the holy in the common, we live a sacramental Christmas.

Because our secular and religious cultures place so much emphasis on Christmas, it's easy for us to miss the Festival of the Epiphany. Celebrated on January 6 (transferred to the first Sunday in January on some church calendars), the Gospel lesson is always Matthew's story of the visit of the Magi to the infant Jesus (Matt. 2:1-12).

An epiphany is a "showing forth," a "making manifest." One tradition combines remembering the visit of the Magi with recalling Jesus' baptism and his first miracle at the wedding in Cana of Galilee, for in all of these events God's presence in Jesus is shown forth.

When the eyes of the disciples were opened at that table in Emmaus, that moment became an epiphany. In the title of this chapter, we have used the word *epiphany* to refer to all those times and seasons we recognize as sacramental.

This showing forth of God's presence certainly must be the primary theme of Epiphany times. Yet as we read the story of the Magi's visit to the infant Jesus, we find another dimension rich with meaning—the gifts of gold, frankincense, and myrrh. Gold is the easy one to understand; it symbolizes material wealth. Upon investigation, we learn that frankincense was used as incense in worship practices of the ancient Near East. Myrrh seems a strange gift for a baby, for it was used as an aromatic to place on a dead body in preparation for burial.

What gifts can we bring as sacrifices of praise and thanksgiving in response to the gift of the holy during the Epiphany times of life? We offer what we have—our possessions (gold), our worship (frankincense), and how we live our lives and die our deaths (myrrh). Christina Rossetti expressed this concept beautifully in one of our favorite carols:

> What can I give him, poor as I am?
> If I were a shepherd, I would bring a lamb;
> If I were a wise man, I would do my part;
> Yet what I can I give him: give my heart.[5]

In times when we are keenly aware of God's great gift to us and we offer up all of ourselves as our grateful response, we celebrate Epiphany.

When our eldest son and daughter-in-law lived in Spain, they discovered that Epiphany there was a much more festive celebration than Christmas. Epiphany was the time for processions and gift giving and great joy.

We miss something important when we rush our Christmas trees to the curb and heave a sigh of relief that "Christmas is over!" as soon as the last guest is out the door. The church has a great opportunity to reclaim the "twelve days of Christmas"[6] that conclude with the celebration of Epiphany. By January 6 our secular culture is exhausted and seemingly glad to let us go about our faith journey in peace! If we could learn to keep Advent and to celebrate Christmas as we reclaim the stories of our faith, then we could enjoy the feasts and festivity of Epiphany. We could teach our children to keep their eyes open for Epiphany moments in their lives when they see God and to give themselves in return, for the gift of one's self is the greatest Christmas present of all, as God showed us in the gift of Jesus.

## Lent

After the ashes remind us of our mortality and our need to repent and believe the good news, we hear the stories of Jesus' temptation. In these ritual acts and stories, we confront our own times of wrestling and our encounters with paradoxes beyond our understanding. (We explored this idea together in chapter 3.) We probably think of Lent as a time of preparation for observing God's saving act through Jesus on Good Friday.

While these themes are clearly present, the early church understood Lent more comprehensively. Lent was a time when the catechumens—those to be baptized at

Easter—prepared for their baptism. We recapture that understanding of Lent in the Lenten lectionary readings. For with the catechumens, the entire church prepares for the renewal of our baptismal covenant. And that means that our preparation is not just for remembering the crucifixion of Jesus on Good Friday but also for recalling the Resurrection event of Easter. Once again, death and resurrection command our attention. This wrestling with death and resurrection characterizes the depth dynamic of Lent.

Combining Jesus' own time of wrestling with our preparation to renew our baptismal covenant, we become aware of times when we wrestle with life-and-death decisions, challenges that involve our whole being. Whenever our whole life is on the line—what we will do, where we will live, with whom we will covenant—we find ourselves potentially heading into a Lenten journey. When we become aware of the enormity of the possible consequences of our choices and know that we wrestle in the presence of God, we are living in Lent.

Dietrich Bonhoeffer taught at an "illegal" seminary of the Confessing Church in Germany after the Nazis banned such activity. One condition of this house of study that distinguished it from a "legitimate" school was that it could not (in other words, should not) give university exams. One of the courses Bonhoeffer taught there was New Testament Greek. When the students arrived at the final class, a school bus awaited them. As the bus drove off, Bonhoeffer handed out the final exam. After the class had ridden through the countryside long enough to complete the exam, he collected the results and put them in his briefcase.

When the Gestapo forced the bus to stop, he told them the class had been on a field trip. After the official left, a student heard Bonhoeffer say under his breath, "Love must be inventive!"[7] We believe that as Bonhoeffer wrestled with how to be faithful to God, his students, and his church in the face of great danger, he experienced the depth dynamic of Lent.

## Holy Week

Holy Week begins with Palm Sunday (now called Passion/Palm Sunday). Most Palm Sunday services start with a celebration of Christ's Triumphal Entry as children and sometimes the whole congregation enter the sanctuary waving palms. Our observance of the church year now recognizes that we cannot celebrate Palm Sunday with integrity apart from Jesus' suffering and death. Many churches end this Sunday morning service with the shadow of the cross looming over congregants as they read the Passion story. We lose much of the sacramental potential for Passion/Palm Sunday if we celebrate only the palms and the children and crowd's shouting "hosanna!"

The meaning of the word *hosanna* provides a clue to the deeper meaning of the day. *Hosanna* is the transliteration of the Hebrew word at the beginning of Psalm 118:25. That is, it takes the letters in the Hebrew word and puts them in a form we can read. But if you look at that verse in the Psalter at the back of *The United Methodist Hymnal*, in the New Revised Standard Version of the Bible, or even in the King James Version, you don't find the word *hosanna* at all. Instead you find the word translated as "Save us" or "Save now." Obviously this is a plea for God's saving action. This word is a part of the Hallel psalms that pilgrims recited on their way to Jerusalem. It is not strange at all to find it on the lips of pilgrims on that first Palm Sunday. But in reference to Jesus' Triumphal Entry into Jerusalem, it seems to have a different but related meaning. Jesus is greeted with the cry: "Hosanna to the Son of David! Blessed is the one who comes in the name of the Lord! Hosanna in the highest heaven!" (Matt. 21:9).

Pilgrims have been praying for salvation; God has heard their prayer; now is the time of God's salvation, and Jesus comes to bring it. This combination of plea and victory shout lies at the heart of the inner meaning of the day. One of the few hymns to capture this concept says:

> Ride on, ride on in majesty!
> In lowly pomp ride on to die;
> Bow thy meek head to mortal pain,
> Then take, O God, thy power, and reign.[8]

In those times when saving victory and suffering are so closely interwoven as to be indistinguishable, we live out Passion/Palm Sunday. The cries of pain in childbirth provide a potent metaphor for such experiences.

Often Christians ignore the early days of Holy Week and give attention to what comes before and after them. During Holy Week this year, however, we received an e-mail from our friend and colleague Daniel T. Benedict. He reflected on a verse from the story of Mary's anointing of Jesus in John 12, focusing on Jesus' defense of her actions:

"She bought it so that she might keep it for the day of my burial" (John 12:7). Here are Dan's reflections that touched us so deeply:

> She anoints her baby's skin with oil from the Johnson and Johnson's bottle. It costs $3.29, but invested with the love and dreams she has for this child's future, it is costly as the nard of the Gospels. If you were to snap a photo and look at it in normal light, you would see only the glow of the way things are or seem to be. If you looked at it in the light of Holy Week and the truth we were smudged with on Ash Wednesday, you could title it: "She has anointed me for my burial."
>
> We want desperately to believe that birth is unto life. We want desperately to think that the future stretches out in all directions toward prosperity, long life, comfort, and success. Every achievement, recognition, and hurdle overcome gets woven into this tapestry of invincibility. "You will not die," says the ancient and sooty voice. Like the garden dwellers of old, we buy the package—it sounds and looks good.
>
> Our baptism, with its washings and anointings, looks for all the world like a birthday party. And it is the party of new birth. But the bathing and the anointing, contrary to acculturated Christendom, mark us with the cross, and the event is proleptic of what is to be both an existential and a biological inevitability: "You will die."
>
> In our baptism we are given the grace to recognize that we have been anointed for our burial. We are

given grace to say with Paul and all the company of heaven and earth: "I am crucified with Christ, and it is no longer I who live but Christ who lives in me."

In Holy Week we all dine at the house in Bethany and with Jesus we all receive anew the anointing for the day of our burial. This is not morbidity. It is the weaving of death into the fabric of the hope proclaimed in the gospel—in the cross, passion, and death of Jesus.[9]

Whenever we appropriate this anointing as both sign of our mortality and sacramental symbol that marks us for eternity as members of Christ's own family, we live out that part of Holy Week.

### The Triduum: Holy Thursday through Easter Sunday

In chapter 3 we looked at disruptive discords of life. For the disciples, the day of the Crucifixion was certainly such a time. However, we choose to look at the events of Holy Thursday through Easter Sunday (known as "the triduum"—the three days) as a whole. That larger view is symbolized in the tradition that beginning with the service on Holy Thursday evening, none of the services until the Easter Vigil concludes in the usual way—no benediction, no blessing and dismissal, no postlude. This practice is a way of saying liturgically, "This service isn't over yet; we haven't yet heard the rest of the story." Remember that both in the Eucharist and in the baptismal covenant, death and resurrection are bound together almost as one word: death-and-resurrection.

Last fall Dwight received a term paper from Donna Techau, a graduate student with eight years of nursing experience in intensive care units. In her paper she reflected on baptism as a celebration of the Resurrection (as she says, "Christ's resurrection and ultimately, ours"). She included these excerpts from her personal journal:

My coworkers in labor and delivery, knowing my religious affiliation as a divinity student, contacted me in the ICU and asked me to come. Upon entering the delivery room, I found a tearful young mother cradling her newborn, blue baby against her breast. A distance from the bed stood an awkward young man in a clerical collar, his face pale and tense. She wanted her stillborn baby baptized; his [understanding of the church and of baptism] paralyzed him into impotence. He mumbled something about the function of infant baptism and explained that the child was in no need. He . . . feebly attempted to offer comfort through his words. [The mother] sobbed audibly.

I sat on the edge of the bed and asked to hold her little boy. Rocking his cold, cyanotic, tiny form gently in my arms, I noted his perfection—the details of his hands, his streaks of brown hair. I commented on his likeness to the woman. Her sobs quelled for a moment and she looked me in the eyes. I began to speculate aloud . . .

"For nine months you carried this child in the waters of your womb. You nurtured and nourished him through your own blood. You breathed life into him. Your blood carried oxygen to him, and the impurities and waste out of him. You felt his every kick and twist and tickle. You know him as you know yourself. He is part of you. In the last hours of labor, your blood was spilled for him; your body was broken for him. Hurting and exhausted from your own outpouring of love, you now doubt your own role."

I straightened my back and carefully delivered the child back into the arms of the [mother] . . .

"You have represented Christ to your son. You have participated in his creation, sustained him, loved him, and redeemed him. You are his priest. You have baptized him in the waters of your womb. Out of those waters he came into new life in Christ. Name your son, and pronounce his baptism. You can. You already have."

Her eyes betrayed a look of fear and wonderment. Rocking the baby close, she hesitantly stated: "Nathan . . . I baptize you in the name of the Father, and of the Son, and of the Holy Spirit." She smiled through her tears.

Laying my hands on the form in her arms, together we delivered her son into the care of the heavenly Father. In simple unison we prayed together: "Into your hands we commit Nathan Allan Linden."[10]

Here death and resurrection were intimately woven together in the fabric of life. Every baptism and Eucharist reminds us of death and resurrection. And when, in the cadence of our daily lives, that kind of sacramental reality breaks in upon us, we are living into and out of the death-and-resurrection dynamic of the triduum.

## The Great Fifty Days

In chapter 4, we pointed to seasons of revealing resurrection, times when we are able to dance on the gravestones. And in chapter 7, we noted the practice of the early church of using the Great Fifty Days between Easter and Pentecost as a time for "mystagogy"—uncovering the dynamics implicit in our moments of mystery, the "mountaintop experiences" that are Emmaus epiphanies for us in ways we cannot ignore.

In a way, this whole book is about mystagogy, uncovering (but not doing away with) the mysteries that give life sacramental meaning, often through gifts of syncopated grace. Sometimes, however, the cadence of a part of life itself becomes a season of mystagogy.

Dwight had a time of mystagogy just before Christmas last year. It is not an event of which he is proud. In fact, he has resisted telling the story in previous chapters. However, sometimes we ignore the nudging of the Spirit at our peril!

We've already told you something about Epworth—our inner-city, multiethnic congregation in Chicago. It still holds an annual Christmas program. Children from the tutoring program and Sunday school participate and bring their friends and families. Many rarely, if ever, attend church at any other time. No rehearsal takes place before the program; tutors are too busy helping children meet academic expectations to deal with a "pageant" rehearsal, and this large group of children has never before met together in one place at the same time. The plan calls for different age groups to meet in different rooms and dress in costumes that several members of the congregation have lovingly made. An adult with each group tells them when to come on, where to go, what to do, and when to leave. Add to this recipe for chaos the ingredient of early teens bringing boyfriends and girlfriends—most of whom are in that early adolescent period of giggly embarrassment.

For this story to make sense, you have to know that Dwight was raised on carefully rehearsed, beautifully executed, lovely and meaningful Advent services and Christmas programs. As both a minister of music and a pastor, he helped prepare and lead them. We served congregations where parents brought children to church for rehearsals and Sunday school teachers helped the children learn their parts. Nothing in forty years of ministry prepared him for this program.

The noise level was unbelievable. We're not talking about a gentle undercurrent of sound; at one point in the program, the reading of two women couldn't be heard past the third pew. Dwight was supposed to be emcee. He made two futile trips to the back of the sanctuary in an attempt to quiet things down. He gave up. The program went on.

The Holy Family entered: they were portrayed by two African Americans in their early teens and the newest baby in the congregation (who happened to be Caucasian). All three of them had been among the eleven persons baptized two Sundays earlier. The preschool and elementary "angels" appeared. A large group of older elementary shepherds entered and crowded around the Holy Family.

Dwight managed to keep it together until the three junior-high Magi came down the aisle as a trio of three girls sang the stanzas of "We Three Kings" and the congregation joined in the refrain. Well, the girls were *supposed* to sing the stanzas. Actually they sang the first two lines (quite nicely, by the way), but on each stanza they dissolved into uncontrollable giggles that their microphones amplified, which caused them to laugh even harder. Dwight couldn't take it. He handed his bulletin to Linda and whispered: "I've had it! God has a terrible sense of humor!" And he sat stiffly in the pew, knowing that this Christmas pageant was out of his control. The noise, confusion, and giggles became disruptive discords, and he faced a crisis of faith. Dwight's soul anguished deeply. He had to face the possibility that he was more committed to the holiness of beauty than the beauty of holiness.

In this moment of crisis, the hymn reached the final refrain: "O—star of wonder, star of light . . ." But Dwight sat stiffly in the first pew—not singing at all. A twelve-year-old shepherd in front of him looked Dwight right in the eye and began directing him with his staff. What could Dwight do? He had to sing. But he still felt like the program was God's joke on him.

The mystagogical season began with the shepherd's directing Dwight to sing and continued afterward in fellowship hall. "No one can accuse that of being sanitized religion," a friend observed. "Come to think of it, this is probably closer to the scene in that first Bethlehem than anything I've ever experienced in church," Linda responded. "How are you doing?" we asked our new pastor. "I'm in shock," she replied.

Then in a frenzy of excitement, Santa Claus entered. We're not big fans of Santa Claus at church Christmas programs, you see. The noise still was deafening as several church members sought to have the children line up by age. As one little girl glimpsed Santa, we heard her say, "Look, look! Santa Claus is our color this year." And he was—a bright and gifted African-American teen was filling in for our regular Santa, who had pneumonia. His mother said he talked more that night than he had for the rest of the year. What he said made a difference. He took his role seriously!

"How are you doing in school?" Alex asked quietly as a wide-eyed seven-year-old sat on his knee. "Oh, okay, I guess," came the answer. "Well, you know," Alex said in a wise, kind voice, "that's not good enough for Santa Claus. Santa Claus wants you to do your very best. Can you do that?" And on and on he went, counseling, giving support, nourishing. And in his words the sacrament of God's amazing love in and among us—even in the stable places of our lives—became amazingly clear.

"I tell this story," says Dwight, "not because of what I felt, but because of what I learned. It was a time of mystagogy for me." Of course, he did recover and we continued to be a part of Christ's body at Epworth in spite of those times that made us uncomfortable. Next Christmas we hope to minimize some of the chaos without robbing the event of its spontaneity and excitement. But we are also learning—contrary to our middle-class, Midwestern upbringing—that chaos can be holy! Whenever such a situation occurs and we recognize the sacramental in the mystery and paradox of our lives, we are living the dynamic of the Great Fifty Days.

## Pentecost

In chapter 6, we discussed the nature of Pentecost power. At times the Holy Spirit empowers us for ministry, guiding and directing us in paths of service and ministry and mission. These times of Spirit empowerment become our "apostolate"—what God's Spirit sends us forth to do.

Such seasons of our lives often bring us face-to-face with the fact that God does not call all of us to the same task, nor does God give everyone the same mission. Since God is One and we are sure of our own mission, we tend to assume that everyone else should also fit into that design.

Last fall, we went to Northern Ireland for a conference on children in the church. Johnston McMasters, a good friend of ours, has worked with youth from the Protestant and Roman Catholic communities in Northern Ireland, seeking to bridge the centuries-old chasm between them. He led a workshop on helping children understand Christian differences.

Johnston observed that differences are built into the structure of the cosmos, that they are part of God's creative grace. A square foot of topsoil one and a half inches deep contains more than 1,300 different life forms, all interconnected. Similarly, in music, you can't have harmony without difference. He went on to talk about how to confront differences honestly and about how parents can help children live with the differences they will encounter.

We sometimes focus on the fact that when Pentecost power came to the early church, "they were all together in one place" (Acts 2:1b). In our attention to the witness that all those present "from every nation under heaven" heard the message, we may miss the testimony that "each one heard them speaking in the native language of each" (Acts 2:5-6). Rather than obliterating difference, the Holy Spirit honors it!

Jesus called Matthew and Zacchaeus to different tasks, although they shared the same occupation. Matthew was to leave his occupation as a tax collector and follow Jesus, while Zacchaeus was to return to his work as a tax collector, making amends to those he cheated. When we firmly commit ourselves to one way of living out the gospel and encounter someone who is equally certain that God calls him or her in quite an opposite way, we sometimes have trouble appreciating that different perspective. One of the lessons of Pentecost is this: The Holy Spirit calls us to listen and learn from persons who differ from us, even as we hope they will listen and learn from us. This kind of interchange requires a sense of humility that allows God to be the judge and to provide each of us with correctives as together we strive to be lights to the nations—to offer hope and compassion and to work for justice and peace.

## Divergent Dynamics

So it is that:
- When life seems mundane and we put one foot

in front of the other to do what needs doing, we are in ordinary time.

- When we long for situations to be different, when we watch and wait, we are an Advent people.
- When we recognize the presence of the holy in the ordinary, we celebrate Christmas.
- When a sense of the sacramental breaks into our lives and we respond by offering our material wealth, our worship, our lives, and our deaths, we live an Epiphany life.
- When we wrestle with life-and-death decisions, seeking to live out our baptism, we are in Lent.
- When saving victory and suffering are closely interwoven, we live in resonance with Passion/ Palm Sunday.
- When death-and-resurrection become one word and we are able to dance on gravestones without ignoring them, we live as Easter people.
- When the dynamics of our mountaintop experiences are uncovered, we experience the meaning of the Great Fifty Days.
- When we are aware that the Holy Spirit empowers us and sends us forth for service, ministry, and mission; recognizing both the diversity and unity of God's people, we become Pentecost people.

God's syncopated grace, resonating with the festivals and seasons of the church year, punctuates the sacramental times and seasons of our lives. However, our experience shows that these syncopations don't happen neatly. Some times may be primarily Advent or Lent or ordinary time seasons for us, but often one part of our lives may be in one season while another seems to be playing a different melody. We may find ourselves involved at work in justice making and feel affirmed as we seek to provide a life-giving product or service. At the same time, our marriage or another important relationship may be careening toward a crisis. What, then, can we do?

Just as Pentecost helps us value difference, so the various times and seasons of our lives can be brought into a kind of harmony of relatedness when we see them as sacramental. In and through these patterns, we become aware of the presence of the living God at work in us and in everything around us, transforming us and our communities of faith into God's kin-dom. We may be empowered to live with the tensions in our lives in creative, healing ways because we recognize God's care and syncopated grace at work in both the painful and the productive places in our lives.

Certainly many persons find the joy and expectation of Advent difficult because of their own life experiences. Perhaps a loved one died near Christmas, or they are divorced and their children do not live with them to share what used to be a joyous time. They may be terminally ill or suffering from depression. Some congregations have instituted a service of "The Longest Night" on December 21 to help people name and deal with the pain they feel during this season when the dominant message is one of joy and hope. Encouraging people to name their own experience and finding ways to acknowledge it ritually are means we can use to empower individuals to acknowledge and claim the conflicting dynamics in their lives.

We discover that even when divergent dynamics occur in the times and seasons of our lives, they are all part of one great sacramental unity. In the liturgical year, the seasons interpret one another. We understand ordinary time in light of the death-and-resurrection focus of the three holy days. During Lent we discover the implications of Pentecost. We remember the manger because of the cross, and Friday is Good Friday because of the Easter faith in which we remember the Christmas affirmation that "God so loved the world that [God] gave [God's] only Son." We live through all these times and seasons with the Advent hope of pilgrims who are on the way toward the final consummation of eternal life with God.

And so it is in the times and seasons of our own lives. Whether in the persistent patterns that we come to recognize as sacramental or during our experiences of God's syncopated grace, we find them interpreting one another. We can live through the grief-filled pain of the first Christmas without our loved one because of the Easter moments of life. In the midst of our highest joy, we carry our deepest pain.

In our baptism, we are made part of Christ's saving action from creation to final consummation.[11] All our times and seasons can be seen in light of God's mighty acts in Jesus Christ, a continual Eucharist in which we offer up to God what we have received and discover that God gives it back to us again, transfigured. With new eyes to see and ears to hear, we become aware of the depth dynamics of God's syncopated grace.

## Appropriating Syncopated Grace

If we recognize the basic patterns of life as sacramental, however, we are also called upon to be alert to moments of God's syncopated grace. When these surprises come, such as when a youth directs a grumpy old man to sing, God gets our attention and reminds us of the sacramental potential of every time and place. The celebrations, times, and seasons of the church year help us turn our journey into pilgrimage. To do that, we must remember and sing and pray and hope.

During Holy Week, we stood in The Museum of Indian Arts and Culture in Santa Fe, New Mexico, pondering the words of Luci Tapahonso, inscribed on a wall:

> We must remember the worlds our ancestors traveled.
> Always wear the songs they gave us.
> Remember we are made of prayers.
> Now we leave wrapped in blankets of love and wisdom.[12]

# Notes

1. See Acts 10 for an account of Peter's vision and then his visit to Cornelius.

2. Over twenty years ago, we attended a meeting of the Christian Educators Fellowship in Glorieta, New Mexico. Dwight went to a workshop led by Elizabeth Box Price that introduced us to this perspective. John and Elizabeth have become good friends and colleagues, and we are grateful to them for the gift of planting the seed that has given rise to our understanding of the relationship between the church year and the seasons of our lives.

3. Laurence Hull Stookey, *Calendar: Christ's Time for the Church* (Nashville, Tenn.: Abingdon Press, 1996), 134.

4. See the development of this idea in Claus Westermann, *Blessing in the Bible and the Life of the Church,* trans. Keith Crim (Philadelphia: Fortress Press, 1978).

5. Final stanza of "In the Bleak Midwinter" by Christina G. Rossetti (1872) in *The United Methodist Hymnal* (Nashville, Tenn.: The United Methodist Publishing House, 1989), No. 221.

6. The twelve days of Christmas are known primarily because of the song that touts such gifts as ten lords a-leaping, five golden rings, and a partridge in a pear tree.

7. Hans Wagner, now deceased, who served as pastor of St. John's Lutheran Church in El Cajon, California, shared this personal memory with ELCA Pastor John Manz. It is reported in the *Newsletter of the International Bonhoeffer Society,* No. 75, February 2001, 1.

8. Hymn text by Henry H. Milman (1791-1868) in *The Book of Hymns* (Nashville, Tenn.: The United Methodist Publishing House, 1966), No. 425.

9. Daniel T. Benedict, Order of Saint Luke, "For the Day of My Burial." Unpublished. Used with deep gratitude by permission of the author.

10. Donna Techau, personal journal, entry dated 1-26-2000. Names have been changed to protect privacy. Italics hers. Used with deep gratitude by permission of the author.

11. In Christian tradition, this is known as the paschal mystery.

12. *Here, Now and Always*, 88. Reprinted by permission of the Museum of Indian Arts and Culture and the Museum of New Mexico Press.

# A Guide for Further Exploration

Since the publication of *Sacramental Living* (Upper Room Books, 1999), God has gifted us with many wonderful conversations with friends who also seek to be pilgrims on the Way. These conversations, our reading, teaching and learning with our students, and sixty-something years of life experience (each!) have led us once again to share with our reader friends our pilgrimage as we seek to live sacramentally.

In this book we sought to focus on the multitude of ways God's grace breaks into our lives in both expected and unexpected times and seasons. We find ourselves more and more drawn to the stories of scripture and the Psalms, and we are learning to look at them from different angles, seeking to discern what Jesus might say to us today through scripture. In a culture that highly overvalues individuality, the centrality of faith communities—especially the church as the body of Christ—seems increasingly crucial.

## Perspectives on scripture

Brown, Robert McAfee. *Unexpected News: Reading the Bible with Third World Eyes*. Philadelphia: Westminster John Knox Press, 1984.

Brueggemann, Walter. *The Creative Word: Canon As a Model for Biblical Education*. Philadelphia: Fortress Press, 1982.

_____. *Praying the Psalms*. Winona, Minn.: St. Mary's Press, 1993.

Green, Barbara. *Like a Tree Planted: An Exploration of the Psalms and Parables through Metaphor*. Collegeville, Minn.: The Liturgical Press, 1997.

Hanson, Paul D. *The People Called: The Growth of Community in the Bible*. San Francisco: Harper and Row, 1986.

Herzog, William R. II. *Parables As Subversive Speech: Jesus As Pedagogue of the Oppressed*. Louisville, Ky.: Westminster John Knox Press, 1994.

## Seeing the sacred in the ordinary, learning to live creatively, and learning to be blessed by difference

Bass, Dorothy C. *Receiving the Day: Christian Practices for Opening the Gift of Time.* San Francisco: Jossey-Bass, 2000.

Bender, Sue. *Everyday Sacred: A Woman's Journey Home.* San Francisco: HarperSanFrancisco, 1995.

Cox, Harvey. *Many Mansions: A Christian's Encounter with Other Faiths.* Boston: Beacon Press, 1988.

Eck, Diana L. *A New Religious America: How a "Christian Country" Became the World's Most Religiously Diverse Nation.* San Francisco: HarperSan Francisco, 2001.

Hull, John M. *On Sight and Insight: A Journey into the World of Blindness.* Rockport, Mass.: Oneworld Publications, 1997.

Law, Eric H. F. *Inclusion: Making Room for Grace.* St. Louis, Mo.: Chalice Press, 2000.

_____. *Sacred Acts, Holy Change: Faithful Diversity and Practical Transformation.* St. Louis, Mo.: Chalice Press, 2001.

Lindbergh, Anne Morrow. *Gift from the Sea.* New York: Pantheon Books, 1991.

Richardson, Jan L. *Sacred Journeys: A Woman's Book of Daily Prayer.* Nashville, Tenn.: Upper Room Books, 1995.

## For a deeper understanding of the nature of sabbath and the role it plays in our faith pilgrimages

Bass, Dorothy C. "Keeping Sabbath." In *Practicing Our Faith: A Way of Life for a Searching People.* Edited by Dorothy C. Bass. San Francisco: Jossey-Bass, 1997.

Heschel, Abraham Joshua. *The Sabbath.* New York: Farrar, Straus and Giroux, 1951.

## Understanding what it means to be a pilgrim and the significance of faith pilgrimage

Mandela, Nelson. *Long Walk to Freedom: The Autobiography of Nelson Mandela.* New York: Little, Brown and Company, 1995.

Palmer, Martin and Nigel Palmer. Text by Paul Saunders. *The Spiritual Traveler: England, Scotland, Wales: The Guide to Sacred Sites and Pilgrim Routes in Britain*. Mahwah, N.J.: Paulist Press, 2000, especially page 75.

## Understanding what it means to live sacramentally

Bass, Dorothy C. *Practicing Our Faith: A Way of Life for a Searching People*. San Francisco: Jossey-Bass, 1997.

Boff, Leonardo. *Sacraments of Life, Life of the Sacraments*. Portland, Ore.: Oregon Catholic Press, 1987.

Bonhoeffer, Dietrich. *Letters and Papers from Prison*. New York: Simon and Schuster Trade, 1997.

Chauvet, Louis-Marie. *The Sacraments: The Word of God at the Mercy of the Body*. Collegeville, Minn.: The Liturgical Press, 2001.

Cooke, Bernard J. *Sacraments and Sacramentality*. rev. ed. Mystic, Conn.: Twenty-Third Publications, 1994.

Huck, Gabe. *How Can I Keep from Singing?: Thoughts about Liturgy for Musicians*. Chicago: Liturgy Training Publications, 1989.

Saliers, Don E. *Worship and Spirituality*. 2nd ed. Akron, Ohio: Order of Saint Luke Publications, 1996.

Vogel, Dwight W. *Food for Pilgrims: A Journey with Saint Luke*. Akron, Ohio: Order of Saint Luke Publications, 1996.

Vogel, Dwight W. and Linda J. Vogel. *Sacramental Living: Falling Stars and Coloring Outside the Lines*. Nashville, Tenn.: Upper Room Books, 1999.

Vogel, Linda J. *Rituals for Resurrection: Celebrating Life and Death*. Nashville, Tenn.: Upper Room Books, 1996.

## To learn more about the church year

Stookey, Laurence Hull. *Calendar: Christ's Time for the Church*. Nashville, Tenn.: Abingdon Press, 1996.

# About the Authors

**Linda J. Vogel** is professor of Christian education at Garrett-Evangelical Theological Seminary, Evanston, Illinois, where she has taught for fifteen years. She is a deacon in full connection with the Iowa Annual Conference of The United Methodist Church.

Linda is the author of *Rituals for Resurrection* (Upper Room Books, 1996) and coauthor (with Dwight) of *Sacramental Living* (Upper Room Books, 1999). She has also authored numerous articles and curriculum resources, as well as these books: *Helping a Child Understand Death, Religious Education of Older Adults,* and *Teaching and Learning in Communities of Faith: Empowering Adults through Religious Education.* She holds degrees from Boston University (B.S.), Andover-Newton Theological School (M.R.E.), and the University of Iowa (Ph.D.).

**Dwight W. Vogel** is Ernest and Bernice Styberg Professor of Worship and Preaching and dean of the chapel at Garrett-Evangelical Theological Seminary, where he has taught for fourteen years. He also directs the Nellie B. Ebersole program in music ministry there. He is an elder in the Iowa Annual Conference and a member of the Order of Saint Luke, which he has served as abbot.

Dwight has written extensively on the spiritual life in books, articles, and curriculum resources. His books include *Primary Source in Liturgical Theology, Food for Pilgrims, The Daily Office* (5 volumes), and *By Water and the Spirit,* the study guide for the United Methodist baptism study. He holds degrees from Westmar College (B.A.), Boston University (M.A.), Andover-Newton Theological School (B.D.), and Northwestern University (Ph.D.).

Dwight and Linda have been married for over forty-three years and have three adult children, three grandchildren, and three great-grandchildren. They feel equally at home in the beautiful Black Hills of South Dakota and in the city of Chicago.

# Don't miss this book by Dwight and Linda Vogel

*Sacramental Living*
Falling Stars and Coloring Outside the Lines

In this book the Vogels demonstrate, through moving stories and thoughtful reflection, the truth that there is no separation between communion with God in everyday life and the experience of the sacred in Christian worship, especially the sacraments. *Sacramental Living* is for Christians who want to move to a deeper way of thinking—seeing God's holiness and blessing in all of life.

**ISBN 0-8358-0889-0 • Paperback • 160 pages**

To order, call our Customer Service Department at
1-800-972-0433 Monday through Friday, or order online
at www.upperroom.org.